MANAGING
INFORMATION
NETWORKS
FOR COMPETITIVE
ADVANTAGE

Stephen R. Ives

To Tiina

Published by:

Computer Weekly Publications
Quadrant House
The Quadrant
Sutton
Surrey SM2 5AS

Tel. number: (081) 661 3099
Fax number: (081) 661 8979

Publications Manager: John Riley
Deputy Publications Manager: Robin Frampton
Publications Executive: Katherine Canham

 REED
BUSINESS
PUBLISHING © 1991

A catalogue record for this book is available from the British Library.

ISBN 1-85384-023-8

Printed in England by Hobbs the Printers of Southampton

CONTENTS

LIST OF FIGURES

PREFACE

I wrote this book because I felt that there was a need for a review of the opportunities created by the new technologies of information networking, that could bridge the gap between computer industry professionals and those that will exploit the technology - business decision-makers.

The pace of technological progress in computing and communications over the last decade has outpaced the general level of understanding of how to exploit them commercially. This is especially true as we move from basic, tactical applications to a more strategic use of the technology. The most significant changes have come in the areas of personal computing, local and wide area networking, and graphical-based software interfaces, and those advances are combining to stimulate a totally new approach to information management in organisations.

Within advanced organisations, the ratio of desktop computers to office staff will rise to over 0.7 by the mid-1990s. Eighty per cent of these computers will be networked. This will lead to wrenching changes in working patterns and practices for white collar workers. These changes will be seen as either threatening or liberating, depending on the perspective of the observer and his or her ability to integrate these new technologies with his or her working habits.

Business decision-makers must gain a better fundamental understanding of the underlying networking technologies and the forces of change that are driving them forward. Only then can you become winners rather than losers in the transformation of information-based enterprises that lies ahead.

CHAPTER 1

INTRODUCTION

2 MANAGING INFORMATION NETWORKS

As the value of information rises progressively, and the cost of information circulation falls, the economic equilibrium point will come down to a level where enormous quantities of information can flow. The so-called information society is nothing but a society which has reached this point. The advances in computer and communications technology ensure the coming of such a society, and we now stand in the transition period leading to the information society era.

Koji Koyabashi, Chairman
NEC (Nippon Electric Corporation)

Information is now the largest portion of gross national product in developed countries throughout the world. Depending on the country it accounts for between 30 and 40 per cent of total economic activity. This is a phenomenon that is really quite new and has very significant implications for the way society in general and business in particular will be organised.

Every time we pick up a newspaper or listen to the news we learn about some new computer or communications related development that promises to change our lives. Slogans such as 'information society' and 'post-industrial' society are used to describe the social changes that our recent advances in computing technology are bringing. Whether or not this period of change will come to be seen as being as far-reaching as the Industrial Revolution is an argument for the futurists and the academics.

Marshall McLuhan, who pioneered new thinking about media and communications, declared that the world is in the process of becoming a global village. He believed that communication through the printed word originally led to the gathering of people into cities, but that this trend would be reversed by electronic communications which would lead to the return of villages linked on a global scale.

So far, modern telecommunications seems to be having the reverse effect. For example, most of the world's financial services industry remains concentrated in New York, Tokyo and London. Stuart Brand, author of the *Whole Earth Catalog*, observes that global financial transactions are conducted at the pace of 'a hot New York minute'. Financial traders still work together, packed into crowded city dealing rooms.

The 'global village' scenarios have been based on the assumption that the data networks of tomorrow will evolve in a similar way to traditional voice telephone networks, which developed in response to the needs of individuals, and where each individual had an equal right to a telephone service.

However the economics of data communications will be very different. The driving force will be the pressure to link the computers which handle the rapidly growing flows of business information within organisations.

The Fourth Era of Computing

Since the beginning of computing there have been three distinct technological eras (sometimes called waves) together with a fourth that began in the early 1980s and which is still underway. These eras are characterised by, in chronological order, the mainframe, the minicomputer, the personal computer (PC), and finally by networked computer systems. Their existence can be clearly seen in a graph overleaf illustrating the share of computer industry revenue growth accounted for by each of these different types of system since 1970.

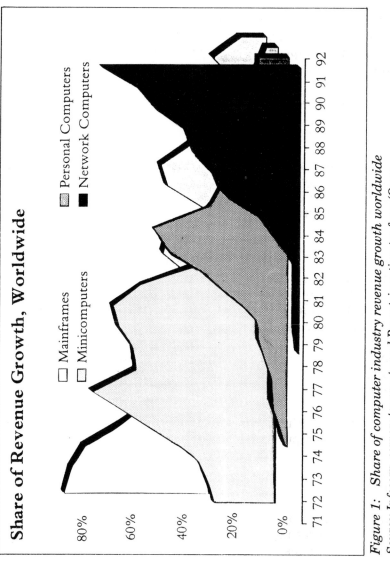

Figure 1: Share of computer industry revenue growth worldwide
Source: Infocorp. corporate reports and Bernstein estimates from 'Open
Systems Strategy' brochure published by Data General Ltd., Brentford

The mainframe era was characterised by computer architectures that were proprietary to individual manufacturers, by software applications developed almost entirely in-house, and at very high costs of ownership. The second minicomputer era opened the business computing market up to a much wider range of users by significantly reducing costs, and greatly stimulated the development of application software by external companies. Like the mainframe era, it was based around computer architectures that were proprietary.

However, the third era - the era of personal computing - was accompanied by the emergence of international and de-facto standards, and by the emergence of 'shrink-wrapped' software that could operate on a variety of different manufacturers' machines.

The beginning of each era was stimulated by two common factors. The first was largely technological: costs were driven down by orders of magnitude in each era as a result of major technical advances coupled with increasing economies of scale in manufacturing. The second was more economic than technological: customers applied computers to new applications, assisted by falling prices and the increasing availability of software solutions for these new application areas.

In common with the first three eras, the fourth era of networked computer systems has both technological and economic undercurrents. From the technology perspective, the critical advance has been the emergence of standards for hardware, software and for communications. Examples of these include low-cost standard commodity microprocessors, standard buses, open systems interconnection standards and standard operating systems. These standards are yielding greater economies of scale and resultant reductions in cost, not only for hardware components but also in the applications and communication software elements that make up an increasing proportion of the total system cost.

The economic forces that have contributed to this fourth era are linked to long term shifts in managerial attitudes and in the structure of organisations, and will be addressed further in Chapter 3.

Information Networks in Business

If you wish to remain competitive in the 1990s and beyond you will have no option but to use the twin information technologies of computing and communications to the full in supporting your business operations. It is hard to find an industry leader in either manufacturing or in services who is not making large-scale investments in information systems to provide the future infrastructure for their business. And growth companies will emerge that change the rules of doing business in their markets by the innovative use of information technology.

Julius Reuter was one of the first people to build a business based on the processing and transmission of business information. In 1849 he saw a gap at the German border town of Aachen between the end of the Belgian telegraph line and the start of the German one. He rented pigeons to carry stock market prices between the two, providing the fastest information link between Brussels and Berlin.

Unfortunately, within eight months, Werner Siemens had closed the telegraph gap, forcing Reuter to shut his operation. He re-established himself in London, buying Stock Exchange information and transmitting it across Europe by telegraph to where it could be sold to companies and individuals at a profit.

In this way the Reuters business empire was born. In 1983 it was floated on the London Stock Exchange at a valuation of over £700 million.

As information becomes the vital commodity of national and international trade, it is natural that we look for tools to allow us to manipulate and communicate information better. Information networks are the channels along which we package and pass this information. They may take a variety of forms, from the biological - Reuter's carrier pigeons of 1849 - to the electronic data highways of today.

These data highways may take the form of local area networks - local to a single location such as an office building or a university campus - or they may span great distances in the form of wide area networks that link countries and continents. They can carry voice or data traffic, but more relevant to businesses is the information content they convey. For this reason I will refer to today's business networks as information networks. Information networks are already being used by today's progressive corporations, and will be one of business's most important competitive weapons in the 1990s. They are being deployed as offensive weapons, to launch pre-emptive market attacks on competitors, and as defensive weapons, to protect mature markets against incoming competition.

As information technology has matured, the budgets allocated to it have dramatically increased. In industries where information processing is central to the business, such as banking and airlines, the data processing budget has increased from around two per cent of total sales to over six per cent over the last decade. These are very significant numbers, comparable with the total percentage spending on research and development or on general administrative overheads in many organisations.

Information Networks as Competitive Weapons

The fundamental justification for investing in an information network is to gain a competitive advantage. This holds true across a wide range of industries.

It is now clear that in the markets of the 1980s and 1990s, we have entered an era of 'total competition', where businesses compete across international boundaries with no holds barred. Business leaders in the US and the UK have come to realise that their place in their market exists not by right, but only by the continued ability to deploy their people and financial resources to stand up to and win against increasingly aggressive overseas competitors.

Coping with international competition

The intensity of competition from overseas firms first made itself felt in the manufacturing sector, where US and European firms came under severe pressure from Japan and other Pacific Rim exporters. Some of the pioneering implementations of information networks in Europe have been in large manufacturing companies responding to Far East competitive pressure. Fiat restructured and rebuilt its car business in the mid-1980s based on major capital investment in computer-aided design systems linked to robot-controlled manufacturing equipment, allowing the same output of vehicles to be produced by a much slimmed down workforce, and at a much higher quality.

In the past, service-based industries were largely shielded from foreign competition because of the need to locate people close to the point of delivery of the service, together with the lack of economies of scale in the provision of services and the government regulation of many service markets. The spread of information technology and the deregulation of many markets is removing this protection for good. Global competition in industries like financial services has increased dramatically, and will continue to do so. Value is created in these businesses solely from the retrieval and processing of information. Networks of interconnected computers have become the 'nervous system' of this type of organisation.

In the UK, much of the activity in implementing information networks was stimulated by Big Bang, the deregulation of London's financial markets in 1985. The entry of US banks into the market prepared to invest heavily in information systems to buy market share, led to a rapid (and sometimes ill-judged) dash to install networking systems. Shearson Amex installed a 1,000 node local area network in their new City location. In New York, American Express cabled a new headquarters building in 1987 to provide 8,000 information network outlets - one for each of their employees in the building.

The benefits of economies of scale

We have always seen economies of scale in manufacturing businesses. In service businesses (where there were previously few scale benefits to be found) the capital investments required to build and operate large networks and databases are favouring the larger firms who are able to finance these systems.

Management consultant and world-watcher Peter Schwartz observes that banks now compete by offering differential service, and the way they achieve that differential depends on their ability to manipulate and manage information. That information is stored on computer databases and is generated from records of business transactions, or purchased from third parties. A perfect example of the innovative use of such information was when Merrill Lynch stole a market by creating the cash management account. This gave the customer one integrated bank account for short term cash deposits, bonds and equities, one integrated monthly statement summarising all account activity, together with a Visa card with which the customer could make normal credit card purchases.

This service required the development of an integrated information system that could record the diverse financial transactions that were possible with such a bank account, drawing information together from several different divisions and different computer systems within the bank.

We can even detect an increasing reliance on information in the mature energy and natural resource industries. Talking about the oil business, where he headed the Business Environment section of Shell's strategic planning group, Schwartz declares: 'you can see it... in the shift of power from the people who find and produce and refine oil to the traders. Producing oil is basically industrial, and all its values are industrial values - things like economies of scale, for example. Trading - everything is information flow, speed of reaction, differences that make a difference, "I know something you don't". Increasingly the game in the oil business is trading. We're going to see that as the driving force in a number of industries. So where before the engineer was the hero that drove the company, now he's a functionary necessary to produce the oil that the trader can really make some money with.'

Changing Attitudes Towards Information Technology

Until recently, the conventional approach to using computing and communications systems in larger companies was to confine them within glass walls, carefully tended by data processing specialists working as a part of a data processing department. Since the first commercial computers of the 1950s, the data processing ethic has reigned supreme. Data has been seen as a vital corporate asset that should be managed centrally.

In many companies there is still a tendency to regard information systems as an overhead cost that should be minimised wherever possible. This is accompanied by a defensive bunker mentality to using computer systems, with data processing staff looking upon information users as the source of a never-ending stream of distracting requests that must wait their place to be serviced.

Slowly the emphasis in computing is shifting to a new perspective. The only rationale for computing in business is to provide a competitive advantage, and the most effective way to achieve this is by implementing systems that fundamentally improve the way information is used by people in the organisation. By this I mean a broad range of people, especially the front-line staff who are the crucial link with the customer, rather than only the backroom paperwork-processing staff. Computing power is beginning to be distributed widely to the desktops in the functional departments where the day-to-day action of the business happens. For this trend to continue, it will be increasingly necessary to demystify information systems by making it easy for people other than the data processing specialists to gain access to the power of their capabilities.

Improving the performance of an organisation

Looking at computers in this way can dramatically improve the performance of an organisation. Chief executives are highly motivated by the need to achieve market leadership, outperform the competition, and prevent markets being taken away from their organisations.

The airline industry pioneered the concept of the strategic or 'mission-critical' information system, which is central to the business, recording business transactions as they happen at the travel agent's desk or check-in counter.

Those companies that were in the vanguard of this movement, such as American Airlines and British Airways, have become market leaders. Their control over the Sabre and Gemini reservation systems has boosted their profits and forced other airlines to compete on their terms, selling on their computer screens.

Enjoying using a computer

Information networks can have other beneficial spin-off effects, in addition to their role in gaining an edge over your competition. It turns out that most people actually enjoy using personal computers (PCs), provided that the software they use is well designed and implemented. A good deal of the repetitive drudgery of office life - proofing letters, redrafting, analysing numbers, 'telephone tag' - can be reduced by the information network. People perceive that value and status is being added to their work, increasing their motivation. As Frederick Taylor observed in his pioneering studies of worker productivity in the early 1900s, people do better work when they are enjoying themselves.

The rapid pace of technology

It is now time to move on to the next stage, to bring the benefits of information networks that have been achieved by the pioneers to the broader population of businesses and public sector organisations. Luckily, the price/performance of computer and communications equipment has continued to improve at an annual rate of over 30 per cent. Pioneer users through their prior purchases have created a volume market within which the benefits of mass-production are being applied on an ever increasing scale. For an outlay of £150,000 today, you can buy the equivalent computing capability of IBM's 3090 mainframe of 1985 - which sold for around £2 million.

Only recently, in the 1980s, have we been able to consider the possibility of providing people with desktop computers. And only in the last few years, following recent advances in networking technology, have we been able to link these computers together in communications networks to become genuinely useful business tools. As with telephones and televisions, the US has led Europe in the take-up of the new technology. By the end of 1988, 30 per cent of US white collar workers had a desktop computer, while the figure for Europe was only 15 per cent. Within advanced organisations able to implement information networks, this percentage will rise to 70 per cent by the mid-1990s.

An irreversible change in working patterns looms ahead, which will ultimately affect all of us who work in offices. The centralised data processing systems of the past were to a greater or lesser extent invisible to most people within the organisation; the same will not be true of the information networks that are being built now and in the future.

The sheer pace of technological change has left most of us unprepared for the changes in store for us over the next decade. The wealth of new computing products and technologies exceeds by far the understanding of how to exploit them commercially. This is just as true within the community of computer professionals itself, where there are many vested interests that seek to perpetuate the centralised data processing ethic, and have not yet learned to live with the implications of the information network.

Making information networks work for you

We who are the end users of computers, including managers, professional staff and secretaries will be the main beneficiaries of information networks. We will need a better understanding of the underlying technologies of these systems, the potential benefits and the industry jargon, if we are to participate effectively in their design and implementation within our own offices. Those of us who have been directly involved in network installation projects have learnt that only when there is direct end-user participation in the design and implementation phases will the system be accepted by people, and be able to deliver the productivity benefits that justify the upfront investment.

The time is now right to try and bridge the gap between the computer professionals and the rest of us who are more and more the direct consumers of information technology. So the purpose of this book is twofold. First, to help you gain a better understanding of the potential of information networks to improve the competitive position and effectiveness of businesses. Second, to give practical advice that can help you to implement these systems in your own organisations.

CHAPTER 2

THE BUSINESS BENEFITS OF INFORMATION NETWORKS

The business benefits that can be achieved from information networks are best understood by first reviewing a conceptual framework first proposed by Nolan, Norton & Co. in 1987.

Nolan, Norton divided the use of personal computers in large organisations into four categories of evolution:

- technical proficiency
- task automation
- business process automation
- strategic systems

Technical Proficiency

In the earliest phase of use of PCs, users must first become familiar with the new technology. Users need high levels of training and support in this phase, as they become proficient in single user applications such as spreadsheets, word processors and databases. The efforts of users are generally not directed towards specific goals, other than gaining expertise in particular applications.

The benefits to the organisation in terms of increased productivity of individuals are low, and do not on their own justify the costs of hardware, software, training and support that are incurred. However, achieving technical proficiency is a necessary prerequisite to unlocking the benefits that come in the later phases of using personal computers.

Task Automation

In this phase, the technical expertise acquired during the first phase is put to use in increasing the efficiency of tasks performed by individuals. The use of PCs is more directed towards applications that have a tangible benefit to the organisation. Typical objectives in the task automation phase might include achieving better business decisions through the use of spreadsheet modelling techniques, or developing a simple database application to bypass the development backlog in the central data processing (DP) department.

Nolan, Norton observed that a ten to 20 per cent return on investment was typically achieved during the task automation phase. Investments in personal computing in this phase are driven by improvements in technology which lead to new opportunities to perform specific tasks more effectively.

Business Process Automation

Once organisations have gained some familiarity with automating specific tasks, the next stage is to identify particular business processes that can be improved or substantially automated. Business process automation is targetted at business activities that are directly linked to revenues or costs, and may involve the integration of several separate business functions within a department. Examples of this include automated manufacturing resource planning systems (MRP) and just-in-time (JIT) inventory control systems.

Automation of business processes is generally implemented within a specific functional department, e.g. manufacturing and is primarily concerned with the streamlining of operational activities. The expected return on investment should be significantly greater than the earlier phases of automation, with returns of up to 300 per cent attainable.

Strategic Systems

The highest return on investment is achieved when entire business processes are automated on an organisation-wide, strategic level. Strategic systems typically function at the heart of an organisation, processing business transactions in real time. Any interruption in the system due to computer malfunction severely jeopardises the ongoing operations of the business. For this reason such systems are often referred to as mission-critical systems.

In order to implement strategic systems, a higher level of insight is required to identify the most important applications of systems and to focus on these. This requires not just top-level management participation, but also the ability to identify key strategic issues in the business that determine its competitive position in the marketplace. To date, successful implementations of strategic systems are relatively few in number, but when achieved they yield the largest financial returns - up to a 1000 per cent return on investment.

The four phases of implementation of PC technology are generally carried out in sequence, as shown in Figure 2. A minimum level of technical proficiency within the organisation is required before task automation can be attempted, and experience in task automation is usually a prerequisite to automating an entire business process. A significant amount of collective organisational learning must take place before the full benefits of information technology can be unlocked. Within each phase, there is a low initial financial return (which may even be negative during the initial installation of the system), followed by a rapid learning curve which then tails off as the financial benefits become fully exploited. To attain greater financial returns, it is then necessary to make the transition to the next phase of automation.

1 Technical proficiency

2 Task automation

3 Business process automation

4 Integrated business-wide
systems

*Nolan, Norton & Co. model

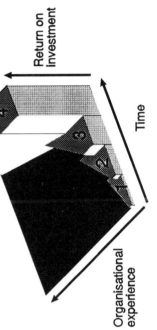

Figure 2: The four phases of application of PC technology in organisations

The Evolution of Information Networks within an Organisation

The benefits that can be achieved from information networks follow the four phases of evolution described by Nolan, Norton. Firstly, some degree of technical proficiency in PCs must be achieved. The subsequent phases are workgroup task automation, business process automation and strategic systems.

Technical proficiency

PCs are generally first used in organisations in standalone mode by 'early adopters' who are enthusiasts in the new technology. They gain a level of individual proficiency in the use of single user software applications such as Lotus 1-2-3, Wordstar and dBaseIII. As enthusiasts they also act as catalysts for the introduction of new technology to other staff within the organisation, although this role is sometimes formalised by the establishment of an Information Centre.

Despite the enthusiasm of these pioneer users, the productivity gains actually achieved from their use of PCs are very low. PCs are used more in exploring a new technology than in any serious effort to support the operations of the business. In many cases, these early pioneers apply their computers to personal office housekeeping tasks that have no net effect on the business whatsoever, with a resulting low or zero return on investment.

This difficulty in identifying a business return from early expenditures on PC equipment, training and support led in many companies to restrictions being placed on the provision of personal computers by senior management. However, it must be recognised that achieving a level of technical proficiency in PCs within the organisation is a necessary prerequisite to unlocking the much greater benefits achievable in the later phases of information networking.

Workgroup task automation

Networks are first installed at the level of the single workgroup or department, serving between five and 50 users, and used to automate specific tasks carried out by individuals. Task automation on a network can deliver greater benefits than on a standalone PC. The network allows information and resources to be more easily shared between users, allowing tasks to be more easily coordinated among group members.

The most basic objectives that can be set for information networks at the workgroup level include the reduction of costs, better quality business decisions, increased responsiveness and increased productivity.

Cost reduction

Costs can be reduced through the implementation of better procedures made possible by the information network.

Examples of this include:

- The preparation of documents using word processing software in conjunction with a shared file library on a network file server. Documents can be easily accessed for revision by workgroup users, reducing the need for retyping.

- In-house production of high quality slides and overhead transparencies, with common access to a shared slide library, allowing the time spent in the preparation of presentations to be minimised.

Objectives of this type, which lead to clearly identifiable financial savings make the cost-justification process, and subsequent monitoring of savings achievements, relatively straightforward.

Business process automation

Once organisations have gained some familiarity with automating specific tasks, the next stage is to identify particular business processes that can be improved or substantially automated through the use of an information network.

When looking to automate business processes, there is implicitly an emphasis on restructuring existing tasks in a way that directly increases sales or reduces costs. A number of different examples of this phase of automation can be given across the full range of different functions in an organisation.

Financial Control and Accounting

All companies generate transactions in the normal course of their day-to-day business. These transactions include sales orders, purchase orders, customer enquiries, production orders, dispatch orders and so on.

The recording of these transactions can be done in batch fashion at certain times of the day, or in an on-line fashion, as the transactions arise. In both cases these transactions are processed by accounting or database software, and thereby entered into a computer database.

For finance and accounting departments, the information network provides access to these transaction databases, irrespective of the physical location of the computers. Financial departments are required to provide timely information to assist senior management in making business decisions.

Decision support systems (DSS) allow financial and accounting groups to interrogate company databases, extract the information they need, and analyse and format it so that it can be presented to senior management. This provides the vital link between the transaction processing systems, so necessary for the efficient day-to-day running of the business, and the decision support systems vital for effective management analysis, decision-making and business planning.

The latest generation of accounting software is developed around a central relational database which allows user to query that database in a very flexible and accessible fashion. Databases designed for transaction-intensive environments in large organisations include IBM's DB2 (for IBM mainframes), Oracle (popular on DEC VAX minicomputers and a wide range of Unix systems), Ingres and Sybase. With many of these products it is now possible to directly communicate with the central database from a personal computer on a peer-to-peer level.

Transaction information can be downloaded in raw or summary form for subsequent processing and analysis using popular spreadsheet software packages such as Lotus 1-2-3 and Microsoft Excel. This capability will allow many individual tasks that were previously performed manually to be integrated into one automated process.

Operations and Logistics

In many organisations the physical distribution of products is one of the core activities of the business, and this must be handled efficiently if the business is to remain competitive. In businesses whose core business activity is product distribution, information networks have become crucial to compete, providing the infrastructure for specialised on-line transaction processing (OLTP) software which controls the distribution process. These systems are vital to allow product inventories to be tightly controlled, and in an era of increasingly volatile interest rates and foreign exchange rates, this control is more and more necessary.

OLTP systems are becoming increasingly necessary to compete in retailing. For example, in the furniture retailing business, it is not generally possible to carry all the catalogue items in stock, especially in city centre retail outlets. Much business is lost when the customer is told that he or she will have to wait ten weeks for the delivery of a dining room table.

With an on-line system, the precise inventory position for any catalogue item is known at any point in time, and can be determined in seconds in front of the customer. A specific item can be located, irrespective of the location of the warehouse, reserved for the customer and an accurate commitment of the delivery time made.

Manufacturing

Just-in-time (JIT) inventory control and manufacturing resource planning (MRP) systems have traditionally been based on minicomputers or mainframes. In the future we can expect such systems to be implemented using client-server database technology on networks. Networks are already being used as a flexible access system to connect minis to terminals or to PCs running terminal emulations.

Networks play an increasingly important role in linking together manufacturing equipment on the shop floor, and linking the manufacturing process in to materials requisition and inventory control. Factory networks are designed primarily to link intelligent manufacturing machines, whereas office networks are designed to link people and workgroups. This fundamental difference in application has led to the development of specialist networking technology for manufacturing environments.

One particular trend in manufacturing systems is worth commenting on here. There is a growing need to link manufacturing networks in companies to their office networks. This allows management to continually collect, monitor and analyse data from the shop floor, for example from particular machine tools, from automatic palette systems, and from barcoding machines.

Engineering and R & D

It has become recognised that research is best done not in centralised corporate research centres but in smaller teams. For this reason, many large organisations have dispersed their research function into several geographical sites, each with a particular specialist role. It is often necessary for these sites to transmit information rapidly to each other and to other functions within the organisation.

The multinational automotive companies have been pioneers in the use of information networks to support their computer-aided design (CAD) and computer-aided manufacturing (CAM) activities.

CAD techniques can greatly accelerate the process by which designers create and modify engineering drawings and product specifications, in a wide variety of activities from semiconductor design to architecture. The use of CAD can often result in the generation of vast quantities of engineering specifications and documentation. Computer-based systems which manage all of this, called engineering data management (EDM) systems, are beginning to appear, helping engineering managers and project leaders to manage engineering projects more effectively.

Ford has developed a worldwide engineering release system called WERS over the last five years, at a cost of $77 million. This system is based on an information network which links 20,000 Ford users in north and south America, Europe and the Far East.

WERS is the world's largest private database, and is seen as fundamental to Ford's plans to move towards the 'world car' concept, with the economies of scale in manufacturing that it brings. The new system will replace six separate and incompatible design release procedures previously used by Ford engineering departments, which have been the root of the problem of international collaboration on common designs.

Senior Management

A category of software - called executive information systems, or EIS - has been developed specifically to provide information query and analysis facilities for chief executives and other members of the senior management team. These systems are designed to be very easy to use, recognising that busy senior executives can invest only a limited time in system training. Because of the limited sales volume potential inherent with such software, prices are high, restricting its use so far to larger corporations.

The objective of an executive information system is to automate the process of management reporting, providing up-to-date, graphical summaries of key business performance indicators to senior managers across the whole range of divisions and subsidiaries of a large organisation.

Sales and Marketing

Information networks are giving sales and marketing departments - which have not traditionally used computing facilities to any significant extent - some significant new tools to increase their effectiveness in dealing with customers.

There are two important categories of system for sales staff. The first, which can be referred to as sales prospecting systems, seeks to bring a level of automation to the process of prospecting for new customers, and managing existing customer accounts. Sales enquiries are recorded as they arise, together with key information such as addresses, phone numbers, addresses, actions taken, actions to be taken and any other relevant customer details. Enquiries are tracked by sales staff through the system, as follow-up actions are made and sales achieved.

These systems are particularly useful in situations where more than one person may need to know the up-to-date status of the account, and where new staff may need to be introduced to an account and its prior history of activity. The network sales prospect database can be accessed simultaneously by multiple users, and all customer activity is recorded in a structured way that makes it more useful both to members of an account team, and to a sales manager who needs to know quickly the background on any specific account. This can provide a degree of protection against losing key sales staff, when valuable on-the-ground account information often walks out of the building with the departing employee.

Against these benefits must be balanced the cost of the system, the training costs of sales office staff, and the time taken in inputting customer information and maintaining customer records. This type of system is best suited to major account management, or in telesales environments where there is a very high volume of client communication.

A second, and increasingly popular application of information networks in sales and marketing is in automating the process of salesforce management. A company's salesforce is most productive when it is on the road, meeting customers in their premises, learning about their needs. To some degree, time spent in the office looking after administration can be regarded as dead time.

A mobile salesforce can be provided with portable computers equipped with built-in modems that allow them to connect to the computer system back at the office. This allows sales staff to send sales order and enquiry details back to the office information system in the evening, from home or from a hotel room. Stock records can be queried at the same time to allow delivery commitments to be made more quickly to customers. And messages can be picked up and sent via electronic mail, streamlining routine sales administration tasks.

Hewlett-Packard, a leading US computer and electronics firm, has pioneered the development and marketing of turn-key salesforce management systems, using their own sales force as guinea pigs. These systems are finding a market in consumer products organisations, such as Procter and Gamble, where sales representatives need to call daily on many retail establishments, and track orders and customer stock levels of large numbers of different products.

As we have seen in the section on task automation, information networks are useful to sales and marketing departments not only in streamlining the processes of customer account management and salesforce management, but also in increasing general responsiveness to customers and in improving the speed and quality of creating presentation materials.

Personnel

There is an increasing emphasis on using computers to streamline the process of personnel management. In a large organisation, there can be significant payoffs from computerising personnel record-keeping by storing personnel records on a network database. Searches on this database can be made to identify staff with particular combinations of experience and qualifications to fill new positions in the company. The process of sifting and responding to employment applications can be accelerated, ensuring that all offer letters go out promptly. The database can be linked into payroll systems for rapid generation of paycheck information. Staff turnover can be tracked in different departments to help the personnel department identify potential problem areas.

The personnel department can be one of the biggest beneficiaries from electronic mail. This allows personnel staff to be contacted more easily by staff, and to respond faster, especially in organisations where they have responsibility for staff on more than one site.

From Departmental Systems to Strategic Systems

The information network, as we have seen, can provide a common foundation for task automation applications and for the automation of entire business processes within departments.

The greatest payoffs in the future will come when individual departmental systems, running these different applications, are linked together via the information network. It is the binding together of the activities of the different functions (or the different project teams in a matrix organisation) which lies at the heart of the role of senior management. In this way the benefits of the network can be extended from the departmental level to the strategic organisational level. In Chapter 3, we will examine these company-wide strategic opportunities in much more detail.

By agreeing common standards for data communication and data interchange across the entire organisation, the groundwork is laid for better and quicker exchange of information between different departments. In this way the binding together and coordination of these different groups can be strengthened. This can be harnessed to increase sales, by improving responsiveness to customers and to market trends, or to cut costs by reducing inventories, or reducing duplication of effort.

The establishment of agreed computing and communications standards across an organisation is a necessary prerequisite to company-wide strategic systems being established. I will address the topic of standards further in Chapter 6.

CHAPTER 3

THE STRATEGIC IMPLEMENTATION OF INFORMATION NETWORKS

Strategy in business can be defined as 'the effective allocation of resources to achieve a competitive advantage in selected markets in order to generate sustainable financial returns which are superior to competitors'. In other words, effective strategy is all about gaining a sustainable competitive advantage in your chosen market or markets.

Competitive strategy is not a new concept. Many of the basic principles were established in the field of war, and have changed little since the time of Frederick the Great, who proved that a compact army deployed according to a skilful strategy can overcome much larger opponents. And so it is in business, where we find many latter day examples of Davids slewing Goliaths.

Digital Equipment pioneered the business market for minicomputers, stealing it from under the noses of IBM, yet were for many years a fraction of their opponent's size. Honda is the best-selling imported car in the US, yet the company started business at the end of 1945 selling small motors to mount on bicycles, when Ford and General Motors between them were selling five million cars per year in the US. The Japanese have been particularly adept and relentless exponents of the principles of competitive strategy in business.

More and more we are seeing information technology being deployed as one of the main weapons by which a corporation pulls ahead of its competition. For every company that has used technology in this way there is an equal or greater number of companies that have been driven to the brink of closure by aggressive competitors who used information technology against them.

Information systems that are used to gain competitive advantage are called strategic systems. Often such systems function at the heart of an organisation, processing business transactions in real-time. Any interruption in the system due to computer malfunction would severely jeopardise the ongoing operations of the business. This type of strategic system is sometimes called a mission-critical system. In the past, strategic systems were implemented with mainframe computers linked to hundreds or thousands of dumb terminals. Increasingly, as the computer industry moves away from mainframe-oriented environments towards environments based on desktop computers, the foundation for strategic systems is becoming the information network.

Examples of Strategic Systems

American Airlines

Airline reservation systems were the first large-scale implementations of strategic systems. American Airlines, with their Sabre system, were the first to place terminals directly in travel agents offices. These terminals could be used to make ticket reservations on any airline, but gave some degree of preference to American Airlines flight information over that of other carriers. The Sabre system cost $350 million in start-up costs, but this investment paid off handsomely as American Airlines took the leading share of terminal installations in travel agents. Once installed, it proved very difficult for competitors to displace these terminals.

British Airways developed a comparable system in Europe, called Gemini. This is now being replaced by the second-generation Galileo reservation system based on networks of IBM-compatible PCs installed in travel agents' offices and linked into the central Galileo IBM mainframes.

American Hospital Supply

American Hospital Supply's ASAP system revolutionised the hospital supply distribution business in North America, and is regarded as a classic strategic systems success story. Distribution of supplies to hospitals presents a considerable logistical challenge to hospital suppliers, who must keep thousands of different items in stock with a next day delivery commitment.

The ASAP system was originally devised not as a strategic system, but simply as a response to this logistical complexity. American Hospital Supply offered a free order-entry terminal to any hospital, linked in to an integrated on-line order-processing, product description and inventory control system.

It turned out that these terminals were very attractive to hospitals and clinics, significantly reducing the burden of purchasing paperwork. And once they had become accustomed to using the terminals, they channelled more and more of their purchasing requirements through the system. As with the Sabre system, competitors had great difficulty in persuading customers to change to a different system.

The introduction and development of the ASAP system is credited with establishing American Hospital Supply as the market leader in hospital distribution in North America, and driving some of their largest competitors out of the market.

The Principles of Competitive Strategy

How can we use information networks in our own organisations in a strategic sense? Before we can answer this question, we need to understand the nature of the competitive forces in business, and the different generic ways that information systems can be used to achieve competitive advantage.

Michael Porter, in his book *Competitive Strategy* has identified five main competitive forces with which any business must successfully cope:

- market entry by new players
- threat of substitution
- bargaining power of customers
- bargaining power of suppliers
- rivalry between existing competitors

To successfully withstand these forces there are three potentially successful generic strategies that Porter has identified, together with a fourth that I have added for the sake of completeness:

- overall cost leadership
- product or service differentiation
- market focus
- alliance/merger/acquisition

Each of these strategies can be used in an offensive or a defensive sense. It is rarely possible to pursue more than one of the first three at any one time. Effective implementation of any of these requires total organisational commitment.

Firms that fail to develop their strategy in one of these key directions - that get 'stuck in the middle' - are almost always guaranteed low profitability. There can be a tendency for firms to flip back and forth over time between these generic strategies - an approach that generally ends in failure.

Overall cost leadership

The emphasis here is on:

- building scale-efficient facilities

- vigorously pursuing cost reductions through experience, tight overhead and cost control, the avoidance of marginal customer accounts

- minimisation of costs in areas such as R&D, service, sales force and advertising

- low cost distribution

The main relevance of information systems to this strategy is to assist in managing costs through detailed financial reporting, and in supporting distribution activities through building efficient logistics systems. Information systems can also help manufacturing companies by designing products for low cost manufacturing by minimising component counts and eliminating duplication of design activity (e.g. Ford's WERS system).

Differentiation

With differentiation strategies the emphasis is directed towards creating something that is seen across the industry as being unique. This can be through design and brand image, through technology, through distribution or preferably along several such dimensions.

Differentiation provides insulation against competitors through brand loyalty and the resulting lower sensitivity to price. The roles played by information networks in supporting differentiation strategies are many.

Creating a unique product identity (e.g. BMW cars) increasingly demands sophisticated and highly integrated CAD/CAM facilities. Creating unique services (e.g. Merrill Lynch's CMA Account) may require the integration of previously separate information databases across a corporate network. Creating a unique distribution channel, as American Hospital Supply did with their ASAP system (putting a terminal into clinics and hospitals to allow them to order products directly) depended on building a strategic information system.

In all cases strong coordination between different functional departments within the organisation is essential and information networks can play a key role in facilitating this. Finally, to be successful as a differentiated company, you need to provide the tools and amenities to attract highly skilled or creative staff. Information networks are becoming an important plus factor in attracting talented people.

Focus

Porter's third generic strategy is to focus on a particular buyer group, segment of the product or service line, or geographical market. This strategy is built around serving a particular target very well, and each functional policy should be developed with this in mind. Focus strategies rely on firms being able to serve their narrow strategic targets better than competitors who are competing more broadly, and who may even choose to ignore a particular niche market entirely.

Focus strategies are pursued with similar skills and resources to differentiation strategies, but more narrowly directed at the particular strategic target. Information networks therefore should be used in similar ways to those outlined for differentiation strategies.

Alliance/merger/acquisition

The fourth and final generic strategy depends upon the forging of strategic alliances, mergers or acquisitions to form synergistic '2 + 2 = 5' partnerships to expand market share, or to fill out a product or service line. Often information technology is seen as a key part of the planned synergy, binding together previously separate organisations into a cohesive, communicating whole. Unfortunately in reality it doesn't always happen that way. Very often the challenge of integrating the diverse information systems between different companies can be one of the greatest obstacles to achieving the required synergy benefits.

There are essentially two main short-term options in these situations: either scrap one party's information system and install your own, or to link the two systems into a common information network by using appropriate bridging and gateway products. In the longer term, merged businesses can build information networks around common computing and communications standards, but this requires a large investment of time and money, and therefore a much longer decision cycle and planning horizon.

Offense Versus Defence

Information networks may be used either in an offensive or a defensive sense in pursuing any particular generic strategy. When used offensively, the objective is to preempt your competitors to gain a strategic advantage. When used defensively, you are trying to reduce a competitor's existing advantage.

Offensive moves generally offer higher potential rewards - but involve higher risks, because you are innovating a new approach, and therefore dealing with a number of uncertain and unknown factors.

Opportunities for strategic systems in service industries

Over the last five years, productivity in service industries in the UK has increased at an average rate of only one per cent per annum. This is despite the significant investment in information technology that has occurred in these industries over this period. It has proved extremely difficult to achieve sustainable increases in productivity in most service industries, especially in those where operations are primarily office-based.

The main inputs and outputs of office-based service operations are information-based. For this reason, you might expect that information technology would have had a substantial impact on the efficiency of these operations. After all, information technology is supposed to be about improving the processing of information through the use of computers.

One of the central obstacles that stands in the way of increased efficiency is the fact that, on average, only one per cent of office-based information is held within computer systems. Of the remainder, four per cent is held on microfiche or microfilm, and 95 per cent is held on paper. This paper-based information must be processed using methods that haven't changed for decades.

If office productivity is to be significantly increased, then ways must be found to store and process information that has hitherto remained outside data processing systems. Often this information is of a nature that defies straightforward storage as data within a computer system. It may contain predominantly qualitative rather than quantitative information. The costs of extracting information from much of the paper held in a typical office, and inputting it in data form into a computer, are often prohibitive.

Document image processing and workflow management

New types of computer systems, called document image processing systems (or DIP systems for short) are emerging that can store information as a scanned image within a computer database. This information can be rapidly retrieved and processed in the same way as data within a conventional computer database. It can be passed around the organisation using workflow management software facilities which are often incorporated into DIP systems.

Using these new types of systems, it will be possible to extend the reach of information technology to a much greater proportion of the information processed in an office environment. Instead of the time-consuming and costly manual transcribing of paper-based information into data which can be input into a computer, the image of the paper itself is scanned into the system using specialised image scanners. Optical character recognition (OCR) software can then be used to index the image. This is done by defining specific areas of the image (e.g. a national insurance number located in a particular box within a form) to be processed by the OCR software.

DIP systems were first used in commercial organisations in the mid-1980s. The early systems were based on proprietary hardware and operating software. This made DIP technology very expensive - with systems costing up to £30,000 per workstation - and for this reason they could only be cost justified in very high volume office transaction environments. Recently, however, the steadily increasing capabilities of standard personal computer technology have made it possible to use high-end PCs as DIP workstations and servers. This has led to a drastic reduction in the price of DIP systems, making them affordable for a much greater range of applications.

Strategies for Increasing Office Productivity

To find opportunities for much greater increases in office productivity, we need to examine what has been achieved in the manufacturing sector, and find lessons which we can apply to the office environment.

Manufacturing operations can be classified in terms of volume. At one end of the scale is the jobbing shop, which is highly flexible and can make a variety of one-off products. Next is the batch operation, where similar products are made together in limited numbers. Finally, there is the production line using dedicated (and usually inflexible) processes to turn out a single product in great volume. The per-item manufacturing cost is highest with the batch operation, lowest with the production line. A reduction in per item manufacturing labour cost of ten times can be achieved by moving from each of these categories to the next.

Service operations can be classified in a similar way. Consultancy can be likened to a jobbing shop, producing a one-off service for a client. Most clerical operations in an office environment fall into the batch category, with quantities of forms being processed by one person and passed on to the next. The clearing of cheques in a dedicated banking facility is an example of a service production line. Different management approaches are appropriate for each of these different types of process.

There are five basic strategies which can potentially be used to increase office transaction outputs without increasing staff:

- Reduction in defects
- Reduction in delays

- Reduction in downtime
- Reduction in paper
- Performance measurement

Reduction in defects

Office workers expend massive amounts of time, effort and money on what manufacturers term 'rework' - doing things twice, dealing with complaints when a mistake has been made, and so on. Up to half of all time spent by office workers may be consumed by 'rework'. In order to reduce it, office procedures have to be made as error-free in their operation as possible.

DIP systems (and in particular the workflow automation facilities within the more advanced systems) will play a major role in reducing rework. Electronic copies of documents are tagged with the equivalent of a work docket which tracks the level of completion of the processing of that document. The docket is set up to prevent the document being passed downstream to the next processing stage until all the required information has been entered into it, and the required sign-off from a supervisor obtained.

Good manufacturing seeks to eliminate poor quality as close as possible to the point where it occurs, rather than to 'inspect it in' at the end of the process when all the time and money has been sent.

Similarly in an office environment, a DIP system can verify the completeness of all documents before they pass from one department to the next, significantly reducing the need to send documents back for amendment.

Reduction in delays

Time is a critical factor in most office operations. If customers can be dealt with more quickly, then the information inventory cluttering desks and systems will fall. Delays can arise for a multiplicity of reasons. Documents may be incomplete. Work is frequently started that cannot be finished. Inefficient information flows between departments and over-complicated processes all act to clog up the arteries of the business.

DIP systems can play a major part in reducing delays. The workflow facilities allow documents to be passed rapidly around the people and departments that need to be involved in their processing. Lost or misfiled documents which are such a significant cause of delay in a larger service provider operation, are eliminated. The progress of documents can be tracked from within the system, to give early warning of problems and reduce time-consuming manual 'hunting'.

Reduction in downtime

Downtime is unproductive time caused by the fact that resources have broken down or are otherwise not available for work. Good manufacturers place a high priority on machines being properly maintained and available. Failure to apply this principle in offices results in delays from faulty photocopiers, fax machines being busy or out of order, or a computer system going down. Wherever possible bottleneck resources should be duplicated, and critical shared computer resources protected by implementation of fault tolerant features.

People, of course, are the key resource in offices. Much labour turnover, absenteeism and low morale results from poor maintenance of people. People need psychological lubrication, in the form of management feedback, training and incentives.

The absence of such lubrication leads to increasing people 'downtime'. The maintenance needs to be focused on the scarcest people resources, rather than just the most expensive.

Set-up time - preparing to do a job - is another potent cause of downtime. Often a tortuous array of information has to be manually gathered before the transaction can be completed. The telephone can in itself be the major contributory factor to high set-up times. It takes about ten minutes of undisturbed time to reach the level of concentration required to resolve many types of office task. Frequent telephone interruptions can virtually destroy the productivity of an office worker, depending on the nature of the tasks they are carrying out.

A well-implemented DIP system can drastically reduce set-up times by providing an integrated front-end to several information sources, e.g. accounting systems, customer databases, correspondence, previous invoices and so on. Workflow management facilities within DIP systems act as an advanced electronic mail system, allowing messages and documents to be acted on by recipients at a convenient point in the day, rather than on a high interrupt basis. With far fewer interruptions, people can complete many more tasks in the same period of time.

Reduction in paper

The waste involved in generating, distributing, reading and disposing of paperwork is terrifying. How much of the paper work flowing round a business is absolutely necessary? How much is routinely read, filed and never referred to again? How much is misfiled or otherwise lost, and will have to be regenerated?

If paper can be reduced, then operational bottlenecks become easier to see - literally. In a factory, work gathers in front of bottlenecks, making them easily visible to managers and workers. In a typical office operation, 95 per cent of the information inventory is stored on paper, and only one per cent on computer systems. In an office with overflowing in-trays and crammed filing cabinets, it is hard to see where the real problems lie.

Reducing paper also reduces the time a job spends in the system. If information has value, then clogged information channels can only delay the time when the benefit can be gained.

A DIP system can eliminate over 80 per cent of the paper in a typical office environment. All paper-based customer information is scanned into a central database. All paperwork-in-progress is managed within the workflow control facilities within the system. In the same way that a mass production environment uses a mechanised production line, a high volume office environment benefits from an automated electronic messaging system which can transport any of the document types needed by the business. This will necessarily need to transport image-based as well as data-based information.

Performance measurement

Measurement is inescapable if management is to be able to pursue a policy of continuous improvement. After all, you can only improve that which you can measure. Performance measures are required for all important aspects of office operations.

The problem with performance measurement in a paper-based environment is the time overhead of measurement itself. Over-stretched staff are naturally reluctant to add to their burdens by compiling time-consuming statistics on their section of the business.

A DIP system, on the other hand, can be set up to generate key statistics automatically. The workflow management system can track the inventory of incomplete documents at each stage of the production cycle. Information inventory levels and document throughputs can be measured efficiently and accurately at many stages of the production cycle, without generating additional work for staff.

The Transformation of Industries

IT has the capability to transform the economics of a number of service-based industries in the 1990s, in the same way that the innovation of mass production transformed the economics of the auto industry in the 1920s.

Insurance companies and credit card operations were among the first service sectors to be impacted by DIP and workflow management technologies. Candidates for the application of these technologies in the 1990s include bank branch operations, legal firms, hospitals and local government. DIP workstations and workflow management systems will become the machine tools and the production line of high volume office operations across a number of service sectors.

The application of these technologies gives an opportunity to many service organisations to gain a major cost and quality advantage over their competitors. In the past, whenever there has been a major innovation in production systems, the innovator has been able to transform the competitive dynamics of his or her industry. This is best illustrated by two separate examples taken from manufacturing industry.

In 1911, Henry Ford was able to produce 78,400 Model T cars with a workforce of 6,900. In 1912, production more than doubled, and the workforce more than doubled as well.

However, in 1913, Ford pioneered the introduction of the moving assembly line, and its efficiencies led to a drastic impact on manufacturing costs and output. Although production of Model Ts doubled in 1913, the workforce actually fell, from 14,300 to 12,900. A decade later, in 1923 Henry Ford was able to celebrate his 60th birthday with 2.1 million sales of the Model T, with a 57 per cent market share in the USA, and nearly 50 per cent of the total world market. His innovation of the moving assembly line was the single most important factor in achieving this market domination, and was copied by all his competitors.

Immediately after the Second World War, Japan began the task of rebuilding its shipbuilding industry. The task of managing the Mitsubishi yard fell to the man who had been responsible for managing Japan's largest aircraft production line during the war. He believed that mass production techniques could be applied to shipbuilding.

During the 1950s standardised, modular ship designs were developed that allowed a large proportion of manufacturing to be organised in a continuous fashion with automatic and semiautomatic fabrication equipment. These modular sub-assemblies were then brought together only at the final assembly stage.

The standardised Japanese designs were rapidly accepted by Western ship operators, and despite rapidly escalating wage rates, the Japanese shipbuilding industry grew to the point where in 1974, it accounted for over half of all gross tonnage launched worldwide. Over the same period, the British shipbuilding industry, which resisted any change in production techniques, was virtually wiped out.

It is likely that new information technologies such as DIP and workflow management will lead to similar transformations in a number of service industries during the 1990s. The time is ripe for new approaches to information management in office-based operations, based on the introduction of strategic systems that will act as electronic office production lines.

Information Networks and Organisational Culture

Strategic systems represent the final stage of evolution in the use of PCs within the organisation, and the most difficult stage to accomplish. Strategic systems require a different approach to investment in networking compared to task and business process automation. They require a strategic vision of how information networks can fundamentally improve the competitive position of an organisation. The implementation of strategic systems requires the organisation to restructure specific activities, not just automate them. It also requires the top-down backing of senior management to be successful.

Nolan, Norton have found a ten-fold or 1,000 per cent return on investment to be achievable through the implementation of a strategic system. However, returns of this magnitude are not easily won. The investment in information networking technology required for strategic systems is substantial.

More important still is the commitment to invest senior management time in analysing the detailed operation of the business, its information flows, and its interactions with the external business environment. Without this analysis, a sound strategic systems direction is unlikely to emerge.

The information network must complement the company culture, not replace it. In other words it must mesh properly with the way things are done in the organisation from a human perspective, so that the particular glue that binds together the individuals and workgroups in the company is reinforced, not weakened. For example, it would be wrong to introduce procedures forcing the blanket use of electronic mail in a business where frequent face-to-face contact was intrinsic to making things happen.

Moreover, we must recognise that no strategic system, no matter how well designed and implemented, can be a substitute for the human powers of business leadership. The moral force exerted by a business leader is a strategic factor that is hard to quantify but easy to recognise in successful organisations. It is the motivating force that builds the belief in individuals throughout the company that what they are doing has a higher importance that is worthy of effort and personal sacrifice.

With any type of automation there is a tendency to focus on the logical, quantifiable aspects of business. A strategic information network should be designed to amplify the existing moral forces of leadership in an organisation, or at least not impede them.

CHAPTER 4

THE INEVITABILITY OF THE INFORMATION ERA

In 1915 Lee De Forest and his associates stood trial for mail fraud after attempting to sell stock in a manufacturing company. De Forest claimed that he had invented a device that would make transatlantic telephone conversations possible. He narrowly escaped prison, but his associates were convicted when the prosecutor persuaded the judge that transatlantic telephony was impossible. Two years later, De Forest successfully applied his audion tube (the first vacuum tube) to transatlantic broadcasting. Since those days the vacuum tube has made possible modern radio, radar television and first-generation computers.

Is Koyabashi's 'information society' a likely scenario for the 1990s, or is it a romantic dream? After all, computers have been used in business since the 1950s, so why should we be predicting a new 'information society' era in the 1990s? The key to answering this question lies in understanding the fundamental technologies of the building blocks of computers. It is the relentless rate of improvement in the capabilities of these building blocks, together with continuing steep decreases in price, that are the principal motive forces driving us towards the Information Age.

The Age of the Information Society

The computer and its generations

The information society will be built with computers, millions of very powerful and very cheap computers. So first of all let's briefly describe the essence of a computer. A computer is basically an information-handling device. When we refer to a computer, we generally refer to a computer system, which is an interconnected group of devices for entering, storing and sending information. Controlling this equipment is a central processing unit, or CPU. This electronic device transforms and transmits information by comparing chunks of data to see if they match. If they match, then one particular sequence of commands will be followed. If they don't match another sequence will result. From this ability to act on the result of comparing chunks of data stems the information processing ability of the computer.

One of the main differences between desktop computers and supercomputers is the speed at which these data comparisons can be made. The power of a computer's central processing unit is expressed in millions of instructions per second, or mips. The £3,000 Compaq computer that I am using to prepare the text of this book is capable of performing three mips. The £10 million Cray supercomputer used in research labs will run at 600 mips.

All computer systems, from Compaqs to Crays, include devices that provide input, (e.g. a keyboard), output (e.g. a screen), internal storage or memory, external storage (usually disk or tape) which are controlled and coordinated by the central processing unit. Communication systems are built from similar elements, but with their input and output stages attached to communications links, and with their processing functions adapted to the job of transmitting data.

The internal memory, the central processing unit and the input/output control devices all share the same basic structure; they are all built from interlinked arrays of electronic switches. The first generation of electronic computers, built between 1946 and 1958, relied on vacuum tubes as the electronic switching elements, and punched cards as the external storage medium.

Second generation mainframe computers, from 1958 to 1964, were built from solid-state switches, called transistors. The transistor was invented by William Schockley, John Bardeen and Walter Brattain at Bell Labs, an achievement that was rewarded with a Nobel Prize in Physics. Transistors were much smaller than valves, generated less heat, and were more reliable. Not only were second generation computers much more powerful (because they could contain many more switches), they were able to store much more information by using magnetic tape drives as the external storage medium.

The development of the silicon chip

Later generation computers, dating from 1964 to the present day, were made possible by the development of the silicon chip by Texas Instruments and Fairchild. A silicon chip is an electronic circuit made up of many individual transistors and other devices etched on a tiny chip made from the semiconductor silicon. It is this unrelenting progress of semiconductor chip technology since 1964 that is the driving force behind the ever cheaper and more powerful computer and communication systems that are the building blocks of information networks.

Gordon Moore worked for William Schockley in the early 1950s. Of his early career, he says: 'When I got out of school (in California) I couldn't get a technical job on the West Coast. I had to go East for my first job. That was at Johns Hopkins University. I was doing basic research into flames and chemical reactors until Schockley called me up one night. When I got into this business, it was a scientist's business. This industry got taken over by engineers later'.

In 1957, Moore, together with co-worker Bob Noyce, returned to the West Coast as members of the team that started up Fairchild Semiconductor Corporation. Fairchild was located in South San Francisco, in the area that came to be known as Silicon Valley, although at that time it was little more than a collection of fruit orchards. At Fairchild, Moore managed the research and development team that brought the first microcomputer chips into the commercial domain.

In 1964, Gordon Moore was asked at a semiconductor conference how many transistors it would be possible to put on a single silicon chip. With tongue in cheek, Moore said that the answer to that question was a formula: 'Two raised to the power of the current year minus 1964'. What he meant by that was that every year that passed since the invention of the silicon chip in 1964 would see a doubling in the number of transistors that could be packed onto a chip. For example, in 1980, the number of transistors on a chip would be two raised to the power 16, or 65,000. The formula became known as Moore's Law, and it held true for nearly 20 years.

In the last five years, progress has slackened off somewhat, to a doubling every one and half to two years. Later on, we will review today's thinking on what the eventual limits to this rate of improvement might be, but for the time period relevant to business planning - say five years - we can assume that the current rate of progress will be maintained.

The invention of the microprocessor and its evolution

After the silicon chip, the third critical invention in the semiconductor industry was the microprocessor. A microprocessor is a programmable information processing circuit that is built on a single silicon chip.

The first commercial microprocessor, the Intel 4004, was developed in 1971 by the Intel Corporation. Intel had been founded as a spin-off from Fairchild by Gordon Moore and co-founder Bob Noyce in 1968. The Intel 4004 had been designed by a small group of engineers led by Ted Hoff. It had the equivalent of 2,250 transistors and could process information only four bits at a time.

The significance of the microprocessor was that it enabled a complete, although basic, computer to be built from only two chips: the microprocessor itself, and a second chip called a fixed-program chip which could permanently store the instructions for controlling the microprocessor.

Millions of four-bit microprocessors are now used today in appliances, calculators, cars, toys and digital watches. For these applications, the microprocessor was a good special-purpose computer, but it was too slow to be much use as a general-purpose commercial computer. More powerful microprocessors which could process eight bits of information at a time were required for these machines. Although the Intel 8008 (announced in 1974 with the equivalent of 6,000 transistors) was not the first eight-bit microprocessor, it was the first with the power needed to build a self-contained computer system. Following its introduction in 1974, the MITS company in New Mexico, which was facing bankruptcy at the time, put together an inexpensive computer in kit form based on the Intel 8008 and which sold for just $395. By good fortune *Popular Electronics* magazine published a feature article on it, and MITS was soon overwhelmed with orders.

The next stage in the evolution of microprocessors was the 16-bit microprocessor. Intel announced their 16-bit 8086 family in 1978, built with the equivalent of 29,000 transistors and operating at 0.3 MIPS. Four years later it announced the 80286 (134,000 transistors and 1.0 MIPS) which was the basis of IBM's PC/AT and the IBM clones that followed it. In 1983 Motorola announced their 32-bit 68000 series, which was used by Apple as the basis of the Macintosh computer. Two years later, Intel responded with the 80386, a fast and complex 32-bit microprocessor that could process between three and five million instructions per second. This is the microprocessor incorporated by IBM and Compaq in their more powerful personal computers.

Looking back through the history of semiconductors, there have been three critical inventions: the original transistor; the silicon chip; and the microprocessor. Each of these have made a real difference to the way that things were done in the computer industry. Of course, there have been other advances, but they have been evolutionary within the boundaries defined by a very powerful technology. But we should not underestimate the importance of the evolutionary stages.

The immense growth in capacity

The staggering capability of the semiconductor industry to keep on delivering twice the power and twice the capacity every one to two years for the same price, over a timeframe now stretching over 20 years, is perhaps unprecedented in any other industry of the twentieth century. It is this ability to consistently keep on giving radically more computer power for the same money which will ensure that society will keep finding new ways of harnessing this cheaper and cheaper power. In the business world, much of it will be put to use in building the information networks that will become a standard feature of the office landscape by the year 2000.

The memory chips used in today's computers typically store 1 million bits of information, and are called one-megabit DRAMs. Four-megabit DRAMs are already freely available to manufacturers and users, and engineering prototypes of 16-megabit chips are being fabricated which are expected to reach volume production by 1992. A 16-megabit chip smaller than your thumbnail will store over 700 typed pages of text. Each year, the cost per bit of stored information has dropped by 30 per cent with the result that total market for semiconductor memory has increased by 100 per cent per annum. Every three years or thereabouts we can expect a quadrupling of storage capacity in the next generations of memory chips.

Getting more transistors on a chip

Looking forward, the key to continuing the momentum of current progress lies in the ability to keep on packing more transistors on a chip, whether we are talking about memory chips or about microprocessors. Individual transistors are etched on the surface of silicon chips by a technique called photolithography, and more recently, by drawing them with a miniature electron beam.

To pack more transistors on a chip, we have only three choices:

- to make the individual devices smaller
- to make the silicon chip itself bigger
- to create more than one layer of devices on the chip

No-one has yet succeeded in creating viable multi-layer commercial devices, and even if they could be created they may get too hot to be practical. It is exceedingly difficult and expensive to increase the size of the silicon chip beyond the one square centimetre of today's devices. A single transistor defect out of a million transistors can wreck an entire silicon chip. In a mature, high-yielding fabrication line, between five and 20 per cent of all silicon chips have defects and are discarded early in the production process. As you increase the size of the chip (called the die size) the probability of a defect increases, as does the proportion of chips that must be discarded, and so the overall yield goes down. For this reason, it is unlikely that mass-produced silicon chips will get much bigger than one square inch in area by the year 2000.

So when we search for ways to put more transistors on a chip, we inevitably fall back to the one path by which manufacturers have been able to make consistent progress; making the transistors smaller. The width of the individual circuit elements, called the feature size, stands at around 1.2 micron (a micron is one thousandth of a centimetre or one millionth of a metre) in the current generation of one megabit memory chips. Intel's latest generation 80486 microprocessor, running at 15 mips, is implemented in silicon of one micron feature size. Engineering prototypes of 16 megabit memory chips are being produced in Japan today with 0.6 micron silicon.

How small can we go with these subminiature silicon devices? As size decreases and density increases, components cannot shed heat as easily, and overheating becomes a problem. Reliable manufacture of objects so small becomes much more difficult. Another problem is that at 0.1 micron dimensions, the space between individual circuit components becomes so small that electrons start to jump unpredictably from one place to another in a process called tunnelling. If you imagine that the electron is a tennis ball that you throw at a wall, when you get down to 0.1 micron dimensions there is a finite chance that the electron will go through the wall instead of bouncing off it. This effect creates spontaneous short circuits in the chip, making its operation highly unpredictable.

Although the marketing executives of semiconductor manufacturers might have us believe otherwise, engineers and scientists have always known that the downscaling process could not continue indefinitely. Until recently, the point of diminishing returns in decreasing the feature size on silicon chips had been estimated at around 0.5 microns. More recent work indicates that the limit is more like 0.25 - 0.3 microns, with an absolute limit of 0.1 microns using traditional silicon technology. The implication is that traditional semiconductor technology will reach its limits in the mid to late 1990s.

Continuing improvement

Even accepting these limits, we can still be quite optimistic about the prospects for continued improvements in the semiconductor building blocks of computers.

First, let us make some conservative predictions about memory devices. With 16-megabit DRAM chips already in the labs, implemented with 0.6 micron feature sizes on die sizes of one square centimetre, we can conservatively predict a 256 megabit memory chip will be achievable, perhaps within the next ten years. This is based on the assumption of 0.3 micron feature sizes, giving four times the device density achievable in 0.6 micron, together with a die size of four square centimetres allowing a quadrupling of the total area of the chip. It is very difficult to envisage memory chips of larger storage capacity than this without a radical leap forward in semiconductor technology.

Looking at microprocessors, we can see somewhat similar ultimate constraints on performance. The power of a microprocessor in mips is influenced by the speed with which the individual circuit elements can be switched - called the clock frequency - and the number of instructions that can be carried out in each clock cycle.

Design simplication - RISC

The latest trend in microprocessor design is, paradoxically, a movement to design simplification rather than increased complexity. For years, computer designers have worked hard to build ever more complex features into their processors. Both microcomputers and large mainframes contain tiny instructions etched into the silicon chips, called microinstructions. Each microinstruction is a sequence of commands for the machine to perform a specific function. Over time, the microinstructions have become more numerous and more cumbersome.

Conventional microprocessors, such as the Intel 80386 and the Motorola 68000 contain over a hundred microinstructions, more than half of which are seldom used. A new school of thought grew up among computer designers that performance would be substantially improved through a new breed of computers known as RISCs, short for reduced instruction set computers. A RISC machine offers no more than 40 to 50 simple instructions, but can execute these instructions very much more quickly. A conventional or so-called complex instruction set computer (CISC) can execute a single instruction every five to ten clock cycles. A RISC computer can execute a single instruction every one to two clock cycles. Because of this, RISC design techniques can potentially offer a several fold increase in computer performance.

Although the term RISC wasn't coined until 1980, the earliest designs similar to today's RISC computers were done by Seymour Cray in the late 1960s for supercomputers. More recently, John Cocke led a group at IBM in the late 1970s that worked on a simple RISC processor architecture that was implemented in the 801 minicomputer. Current RISC concepts based on microprocessors crystallised around 1980 and 1981 with work done at the University of California at Berkeley, and at Stanford University.

Since then, IBM, Hewlett-Packard (HP) and Sun Microsystems have set the pace for RISC development amongst the ranks of the major manufacturers. At a conference in 1984, Bill Joy, VP for Research and

Development at Sun, made a quip that the number of mips that could be squeezed from a microprocessor in a given year would be 'two to the current year minus 1984'.

Joy's restatement and reapplication of Moore's Law to microprocessors brought plenty of laughs but so far he has been proved right. RISC machines will follow Joy's Law for at least the next five years, delivering twice the performance each consecutive year.

The faster the frequency at which you run a silicon chip, the more heat that is generated. Most microprocessors today are implemented in a silicon process technology called CMOS, which results in heat dissipation levels with orders of magnitude less than older process technologies. The smaller the dimensions of the devices on a silicon chip, the faster you can operate that chip before overheating occurs. As we progress from one micron to 0.3 micron silicon dimensions, this reduced feature size will allow the speed of microprocessors to be increased from a typical 25 million clock cycles per second (or 25 Mhz) to perhaps 250 million per second (or 250 Mhz) over the next ten years.

RISC design techniques will allow us to process between one and two instructions per clock cycle, compared to 0.2 instructions per clock in the Intel 386. And the ability to couple several RISC processors together in multiprocessor arrays will allow perhaps a further ten-fold increase in performance. All in all, we can expect to see individual CMOS microprocessors capable of 100 million instructions per second by the year 2000, and single multiprocessor devices that can operate at up to 1000 mips - 200 times more powerful than Intel's popular 80386. But increasing performance much beyond this will be extremely difficult, at least with silicon.

Gallium arsenide - the alternative technology

If silicon is running out of steam, what about alternative semiconductor technologies? Of all the possible semiconductors nature provides us with, only gallium arsenide is anywhere near commercial exploitation. Gallium arsenide devices consume up to three times less power than silicon devices, and so lessen the problem of heat dissipation. Switching and storage times can be achieved that are between ten and 100 times faster than with silicon. However, there are very great problems with gallium arsenide that are likely to limit its application to specialised areas only.

Firstly, gallium arsenide is extremely expensive to manufacture. Both gallium and arsenic are rare elements, present in the earth's crust in minute concentrations - about 0.0015 per cent and 0.0002 per cent respectively. Silicon, in contrast, is one of the most abundant elements.

Secondly, gallium arsenide is very difficult to work with. The semiconductor industry has nearly 30 years of experience with and billions of dollars of investment in silicon fabrication equipment. Very little of this exists with gallium arsenide. Achieving the dense packing of devices on gallium arsenide chips that is possible today in silicon will be a herculean task. For these reasons it is likely that computers built with gallium arsenide processors will be exotic and expensive creatures used in specialist roles such as supercomputing or very high performance network servers. General purpose computers will most likely rely on silicon technology for a long time to come.

Software and its deficiencies

Let's now pause a moment to consider the implications of all this. The forces that are driving us towards an information era are all based on fundamental performance improvements and cost reduction in silicon chips, the building blocks of computer and communication systems. If the rate of improvement is likely to slow down drastically after the next ten years, then isn't the so-called 'information revolution' in danger of fizzling out before it has truly begun?

Well, not really. Although silicon technology is reaching its limits, the same cannot be said for the software that takes the power of the computer and turns it into useful work. Software - the set of instructions that controls the hardware - is the vital link between the business task and the computer solution. In the pioneering days of computing, organisations that could afford a computer wrote their own software, and the spend on software was a small fraction of the hardware cost.

Today, a whole industry has grown up to provide software for users of mainframes, minicomputers and desktop computers. Every pound that is spent on hardware is matched by a pound spent on software. Despite this, there is a consensus in the industry that the capabilities of the software are lagging far behind today's hardware, by perhaps five to ten years.

Software can be regarded as a layer cake. At the bottom, sitting directly above the hardware, is the operating system - the set of programs that manages the operation of the computer. It is the operating system that allows the computer to manage the screen, keyboard, disks and internal memory. Next, above the operating system, sit the software tools and utilities that simplify the programmer's job, making it easier for him or her to create the next layer, the application software, that performs standardised tasks such as word processing for the user. At the top level, there are specialised end user applications that are not standard packages but customised programs written to solve particular business needs, often on a one-off basis within a single business.

The rapidly increasing power of desktop machines has outstripped the capabilities of the operating system to handle this power. Ninety per cent of desktop machines run an operating system, PC-DOS, designed for the original IBM PC of 1981, which can handle only one application task at a time. Multi-tasking operating systems which can handle many applications at once have been used on mainframes for many years, but it has taken considerable effort to adapt this technology to the very different needs of the user of a desktop machine.

Three important standard multi-tasking operating systems are now emerging on the desktop: OS/2, developed by IBM and Microsoft; Unix, developed by AT&T; and Apple's MultiFinder. Much of the power of today's desktop machines will remain unharnessed until these new operating systems come into general use.

If software is to keep pace with the rapid developments in hardware technology, then we must achieve order of magnitude increases in the productivity of the programmers who write system software and application software. The software tools and utilities that sit above the operating system will play a central role in meeting this challenge. We are seeing slow but steady progress in the development and use of high level languages that are portable across different computer hardware types. This is reducing the software engineering effort required to rewrite application software to run on different computers.

In 1965, 50 per cent of US software was written in low-level assembly language which was tied inextricably to specific computers from specific manufacturers. By 1985, 52 per cent of all US software was being written in Cobol, and only nine per cent in assembly language, largely in the performance-critical areas such as operating system software. The increasing popularity of the portable C language has now all but replaced the use of assembly language even in these performance-critical areas.

A third critical area of software deficiency lies in the user interface - the software layer that users interact directly with when they use applications. The user interface styles used by different applications software products are invariably different. You may be an expert in using the Lotus 1-2-3 spreadsheet, but this will not help you a great deal when you wish to master Microsoft Word wordprocessing. To become proficient in a new software application requires nearly as much training time as the last one learnt.

Graphical interface user

The first significant breakthrough in this area was made by the Xerox Corporation, whose Palo Alto Research Centre (PARC) pioneered the development of graphics user interfaces, often called GUIs for short. Graphical user interfaces make use of visual screen metaphors to make life easier for the user. Screen information is represented pictorially, using multiple panes of information called windows together with graphical symbols called icons, rather than the traditional text-based screen presentation approach. Keyboard input from the user is supplemented by a hand-guided pointing device called a mouse.

GUIs are effective because they take advantage of the brain to recognise graphical information very much faster than textual information. PARC researchers decided to model the user interface on an office desktop, making the computer screen look like a desk on which documents and spreadsheets could be overlaid, together with objects representing in-trays, out-trays, folders, filing cabinets and printers. The benefits of graphical user interfaces is discussed further in Chapter 6.

Artificial intelligence

We are also seeing signs of progress on one of the software industry's more intractable problems; the difficulty of finding good software techniques to handle certain business problems that are solved by human experts in an intuitive way based on many years of specialised experience.

When you make a decision to invest to bring a new product to the market, you are integrating a lot of subjective information: market research; estimated production costs; product development costs and time to market; together with your 'gut feel' on whether or not the new product will succeed. Software that can deal with this kind of problem is called artificial intelligence software, or AI software for short. Very powerful and specialised computer workstations have been required in the past to run AI software, but we can now run these applications on standard desktop machines.

Software progress, although it is coming, will be slower than hardware progress, and we can expect to see a 'software gap' for at least the next twenty years. As hardware progress slows, there will still be plenty of room for improvement left in system software, software tools and in application software. So we can expect to see the momentum of improvement in information networks continuing. It will be driven by improvements in the underlying software for many years after we reach the point of diminishing returns in hardware technology.

How will the IT Change Affect Us?

So change is coming, but how and how fast will it affect us? We should remember that human and social factors have a habit of delaying technological and communications revolutions. It took rather long for society to catch up with the invention of the telephone and the television. The penetration of these devices was initially quite slow as people worked out how to fit them into their lives.

In Chapter 3, I discussed how the greatest benefits from information networks come only when an organisation can restructure its business activities to take advantage of the new technology. This takes time; inertia will ensure that many organisations will only restructure when confronted by competitors who have done it first and proved the benefits. And little is known about how to manage the new organisation structures that will emerge. It may well be that, as Nolan, Norton first suggested, those who use IT to create new organisational approaches are essentially writing the book on twenty-first century management.

CHAPTER 5

THE HIERARCHICAL NATURE OF INFORMATION NETWORKS

Computers today can be classified into the following five categories:

- personal computers
- workstations
- minicomputers
- mainframes
- supercomputers

In 1991, a typical low-priced personal computer operates at a speed of one million instructions per second and sells for around £1,000. The next step up is the workstation, which runs at up to 30 mips and costs around £10,000. A typical minicomputer runs at 20 mips and sells for £100,000. A low-end mainframe operates at 40 mips and may cost £500,000; a high-end mainframe may reach 80 mips and will cost as much as £2 million. The speed of a supercomputer is rated in millions of floating-point operations per second (mflops); a top-of-the-line supercomputer can run at 2,000 mflops, and will cost £10 million and upwards.

The Hierarchy of Information Systems

With the development of the newer, lower-cost computers a hierarchical approach to the implementation of information systems has emerged in corporations. At the top of the hierarchy are central computers that are shared between up to several hundreds or thousands of users. Central computers are usually implemented using mainframe or supercomputer technology, or occasionally with clusters of minicomputers.

The next level down in the hierarchy is the shared or departmental system. This typically supports the operations of a workgroup or department of between perhaps ten to 50 people. Over the last 15 years, minicomputers have become the standard workhorse for departmental computing, and in large organisations these are linked, usually by wide area network connections, to the central computer system. Over the last five years, network servers have emerged that provide shared computing facilities to departmental networks of PCs. Network servers are based on powerful personal computer or workstation hardware and are now beginning to encroach significantly on the traditional turf of the minicomputer.

Finally, at the base of the hierarchy are those computers used by single users, called personal computers or workstations. Workstations are simply more powerful and more expensive personal computers, equipped with more memory, and typically provided with graphics and networking facilities as standard features. Personal computers and workstations deliver significantly greater price/performance than mainframes; the cost per mip on an Intel 386-based PC is around 1000 compared to 100,000 per mip for an IBM 3090 mainframe.

This vast cost disparity is driving organisations away from traditional mainframe-based information systems towards information networks built on a foundation of connected personal computers. In this type of environment, minicomputers or network servers are used to support departmental operations, and networked personal computers are used for both end user information processing, and to provide terminal access to the larger computers.

The mainframe is retained only for that job for which it is best suited: the storage and processing of central corporate data. In its new role, the mainframe can be regarded as simply another server on the network, albeit a very large, expensive and specialised server!

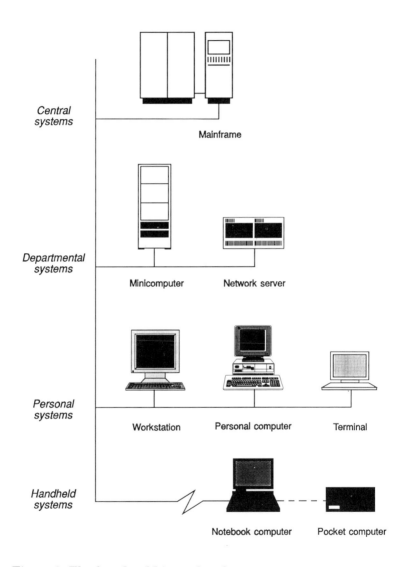

Figure 3: The four-level hierarchy of computer systems

Each of the levels in this hierarchy of information systems is illustrated in Figure 3.

Changing Patterns in the Use of Computers

Within the industry-wide shift towards networked computing environments, there are four important technological trends that can be identified that will have a great impact on the pattern of office work over the next decade:

- The drive of PCs to the desktop
- The emergence of handheld computers
- The trend towards client-server computing
- The trend towards open systems

1. The drive of PCs to the desktop

At the beginning of 1989, 15 per cent of European office workers had a personal computer. In the US this figure was higher (around 30 per cent) while in Japan it was much lower (around five per cent). An irreversible change in working patterns looms ahead. By the year 2000 it appears likely that the majority of office workers in all three continents will be connected to information networks via PCs or workstations.

One of the main driving forces behind the increasing importance of information networks in business is the relentless improvement in price and the performance of computers. This in turn is being driven by continuing advances in semiconductor technology that were reviewed in the previous chapter. When Gordon Moore of Intel made his tongue-in-cheek prediction in 1964 that the number of circuits in a silicon chip would double every year, he scarcely anticipated that this trend would be maintained for the next

35 years. Although the pace has slackened a little of late, with doubling now being achieved only every one and a half and two years, this rate is expected to be maintained until at least the year 2000.

Applying current rates of technology improvement, we can make the following conservative predictions about the price/performance capabilities of computers in the year 2000. One thousand pound PCs will run at 20 mips; £10,000 workstations at 500 mips, and high-end mainframes at 50,000 mips.

The following table in Figure 4 illustrates the cost-justification for providing different categories of worker with personal computing facilities, at both 1990 and at year 2000 prices. Remember that this analysis only includes the productivity benefits achievable from task automation, and not the benefits from business-process automation or strategic business transformation.

This analysis inevitably leads to the conclusion that there will be a clear cost-justification for equipping almost all office workers with a personal computer on their desktop by the end of the next decade. This conclusion holds good even if these computers are used only at the most basic level: for the automation of routine office tasks, to provide a five to 25 per cent increase in office productivity, depending on the category of office worker.

2. The emergence of handheld computers

Beginning in the late 1980s, the ability to miniaturise the key components of computers (microprocessor, memory, secondary storage units, screen) has led to the introduction of true handheld computers.

Work category	Salary cost	Per cent productivity increase	Affordable spend/year	1990 PC cost/year	2000 PC cost/year
Manager	45k	5 per cent	2.3K	5.0k	2.0k
Professional	30k	10 per cent	2.5k	5.0k	2.0k
Secretarial	20k	15 per cent	3.0k	3.0k	1.5k
Accountant	40k	20 per cent	8.0k	5.0k	2.0k
Engineer	35k	30 per cent	9.5k	7.5k	3.0k

Ives & Company estimates, 1990

- Salary costs include apportioned overheads
- PC costs include installation, training, support and financing costs

Figure 4: PC cost-justification analysis

Handheld computers should not be confused with pocket calculators. Calculators are much slower, operating typically at 0.0001 to 0.001 mips and are generally configured with fixed software programs designed for very specific and pre-defined numeric tasks.

A handheld computer operates at 0.1 to 0.5 mips, is configured with 32k - 640kbytes of primary memory, and is equipped with a full alphabetic or Querty keypad together with secondary memory cards for the permanent storage of data.

Only recently have handheld computers been introduced which are able to run standard off-the-shelf PC software packages. Examples of IBM-compatible handheld computers include the Atari Portfolio and the Poqet PC, from Poqet Computer Corporation. The latter machine is the first handheld computer with a full 80 x 25 character screen. Data can be freely interchanged between the handheld and desktop computer, via a serial port in the handheld computer, or by an add-on memory card reader attached to the desktop machine.

The importance of the handheld computer stems from its ability to be carried easily by users outside of office. For people who spend a significant proportion of their time away from their office, the benefits of PCs are significantly reduced or even eliminated if their personal data cannot be carried with them.

In the past, efforts were made to reduce the size and weight of personal computers, and a category of PCs called laptops emerged in response to the need for more portable computing facilities. However, laptops are still relatively bulky, weighing between six and 20 pounds, restricting them to occasional use out of the office, or to particular categories of users (e.g. journalists) whose need for portability is so great that the inconvenience factor can be ignored. More recently, slimmed-down versions of laptop computers have emerged, called notebook computers. These computers have about the same footprint as a sheet of A4 paper, weigh between two and six pounds, and have overcome many of the drawbacks of laptop computers.

Handheld computers, weighing between a half and two pounds, allow the benefits of portable computing to be opened up to any category of user. With their ability (in some cases) to run standard PC software, a wide variety of applications is available: including text entry and editing, spreadsheets, personal databases and dial-up communications software for access back to the office network.

Future applications that will increase demand for portable computers include built-in fax communications and filofax-type software providing diary, task management and database facilities.

3. The trend towards client-server computing

In traditional centralised mainframe-based systems, users access the mainframe through stations called terminals. Terminals have a screen, keyboard and a communications link to the central system, but unlike PCs and workstations they do very little data processing themselves. Instead, data input is sent from the terminal keyboard to the mainframe, and the results passed back down the communications link to be displayed on the terminal screen. The problem with this approach is that the user interface that is provided to the user is necessarily very basic, and any attempt to upgrade this interface incurs large central processing overheads which rapidly degrade the performance of the host computer.

Large corporations first started using networks to provide a flexible and convenient means of connecting terminals to their central mainframes. Devices called network interface units were used to connect up to 32 terminals at a single connection point on the local area network. In smaller companies (and often in individual departments within corporations) local area networks have been generally used in a different way: to provide file-sharing and printer sharing facilities to small groups of personal computer users.

Very recently, a new trend away from this terminal-host centralised approach is emerging, called client-server computing (CSC). CSC is defined as running an application on two systems: the client personal computer or workstation, and on the network server. The client and server computers are typically linked at the hardware level via a local area network. The client application software is able to communicate with the server application via a mechanism called inter-process communication (IPC).

The benefits of this new approach are considerable. Software applications can be written which combine the attractive user interface of a typical PC application with the transaction processing horsepower and data integrity of a traditional on-line minicomputer or mainframe application.

A software program running on a network server that provides a shared network application service to users is called an application server. A standard local area network file and print server is not classified as an application server, because in this case only lower level operating system requests are directed across the network.

Examples of application servers include:

- Database servers - these provide a high-performance database service for network users, capable of supporting many more users than the conventional file server-based database software that is typically implemented on small PC Lans.

• Communication servers - these provide a shared communications gateway for users on the network, with the gateway control software running on the server, and the terminal emulation software running on the workstation.

The topology of a typical client-server system is shown in Figure 5 on the following page.

In many large corporations, populations of non-intelligent terminals are being replaced by intelligent PCs linked to local area networks, running terminal emulation software in conjunction with communications gateway software on the network server.

In most of these cases, the original architecture of terminal-host computing is unchanged, as the new PCs are simply emulating old terminals. Users are not gaining any significant user interface benefits from their local processing power. However, the organisation gains a major future potential benefit; it is investing in a networking infrastructure that has the capability to be upgraded to client-server-based facilities at low incremental cost.

Client-server architecture is beginning to have a considerable impact on database management systems (DBMSes), and will allow significant future improvements in both database performance and user interface. The benefits of database servers will be covered in more detail in Chapter 7. Network-based database servers are likely to render the current DBMS architectures - centralised DBMSes and network file-server DBMSes - obsolete over the next decade.

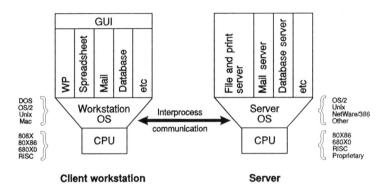

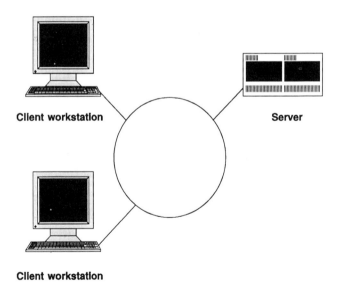

Figure 5: Client-server systems

4. The trend towards open systems

The mainframe and minicomputer systems developed in the first and second eras of computing were proprietary in their technology. This meant that all the key elements of the computer - the processor, operating system, disk subsystems - were specific to the manufacturer of that computer. Sometimes, even different computers within the product family of a single vendor were built to a different technical architecture.

IBM has developed four separate architectures: a mainframe architecture (System/370); a minicomputer architecture (System/34/36 and AS/400); a personal computer architecture (the IBM PC and PS/2); and a Unix system architecture (6150 and RS/6000).

As a result of this diversity, application software had to be developed specially for each individual type of computer. Components such as disk drives and operating systems had to be developed from scratch for each different architecture. This made computers very expensive, and restricted the choice of application software.

During the last decade there has been a profound transition away from these proprietary architectures towards open systems based on components that are common between manufacturers. Open systems architectures include multiuser systems and workstations based around the Unix operating system, together with personal computers built around Intel microprocessors and the DOS and OS/2 operating systems. Unix, DOS and OS/2 are operating systems that run on computer hardware from many different manufacturers. As a result, applications can be developed for each of these operating systems that can run on hardware from a broad range of manufacturers.

Open systems are of most benefit to the user, because they increase the choice of application software, and lead to drastic reductions in the price of the systems. This price reduction results from the economies of scale in the production of large numbers of standard components. Profit margins fall because the availability of these standard components allows many more vendors to enter the market.

During the past decade, open systems have come from nowhere to take over 50 per cent of the total world computer market by value. In 1990, 17 per cent of the total market was accounted for by Unix-based systems, and another 35 per cent by personal computers, the vast majority of which were running the DOS operating system.

Open systems are much easier to connect together into computer networks, because they generally share common communication standards. This is most apparent in the Unix world, where TCP/IP communications protocols have become a standard component of the Unix operating system in most vendors' products. Because communications were not standardised in the DOS environment for many years, there is a greater diversity of networking protocols, with Novell's NetWare having gained the dominant market share. The key standards which provide the underlying technology framework for today's open systems are discussed in detail in Chapter 6.

The Future Role of Mainframes and Minicomputers

Unlike the personal computers of the third era of computing, network systems can take on the full range of applications previously handled by mainframes and minicomputers. What then is the future role for these machines?

Today, mainframes are still the architecture of choice for high-end transaction processing applications where hundreds of individual transactions must be processed every second. Mainframes are also best suited today to the generation and maintenance of very large databases, of the size range 50 gigabytes and larger. While these roles may come to be usurped by future generations of ever more powerful network servers, they indicate an emerging role for the mainframe as a very powerful and specialised network server in its own right.

IBM's own emerging view of the mainframe is that of a central database management engine to maintain central control over database definitions, database development, and network management within a large organisation. The mainframe becomes an overall system 'policeman' for database and network control activities. Many large IBM customers will accept this view and evolve their central systems accordingly. Others may reason that if the mainframe's only remaining role is that of a back-end database server and network manager, then these tasks might just as well be performed by a powerful multiprocessing mini or network server.

As network servers increase in processing power and in storage capabilities, the minicomputer - the traditional departmental workhorse - may be the most threatened by early extinction. Industry pundits have predicted that a two-tier marriage between mainframes and networks of PCs will squeeze out the minicomputer. Others, not least the minicomputer vendors themselves, have expressed a contrary view. The real-time nature of the mini (minis unlike mainframes were never designed for batch processing) and the greater closeness of mini vendors to the needs of departmental users may give them the best chance to preempt other manufacturers in developing the fastest, biggest and most reliable network servers.

One thing is for certain; the competition among computer vendors in the fourth era of computing will be so intense that if the mainframe and minicomputer market leaders fail to adjust to the changes, there are plenty of young, aggressive upstart competitors (like Sun Microsystems, Compaq, or Toshiba) ready to seize the baton of leadership if the established vendors let it drop.

CHAPTER 6

THE IMPORTANCE OF STANDARDS

Any review of information networks must address the topic of standards, since they provide the foundation on which the entire network rests.

The important standards for information networks fall in two separate areas: communication protocols and machine/ operating system architecture.

Communication protocol standards are defined in a number of layers. The lowest layer is embodied in the network hardware, while the middle and upper layer protocols are implemented in software. In addition, there are separate standards for local area networks (LANs) which link computers within a single geographical site and for wide area networks which link separate sites.

Standards have emerged in different ways. Communications protocol standards are being developed more and more on a cooperative basis, by international standards bodies or by committees of manufacturers and users. However, machine and operating system architectures have tended to emerge on a de-facto basis from the offerings of individual manufacturers.

The local area networking industry has largely grown up around the IBM personal computer family and the PC-DOS operating system. While this has set a strong de-facto standard for the architecture of personal computers, the standards for the architecture of more powerful workstations are still in flux. A number of competing architectures including Apple's Macintosh Finder, IBM and Microsoft's OS/2 Presentation Manager and different varieties of Unix have emerged as alternatives, and there is likely to be no dominant standard here for some time.

Why the Need for Standards?

In the past, a lack of standards stifled the growth of networks for a considerable time. Today, however, clear standards have emerged at most of the important network layers.

Why are standards important? A strong standard will attract the attention of a wide range of suppliers, who will make available products that conform to that standard. This will create a wide range of compatible products from which customers can choose. Therefore, standards create choice.

With choice comes competition. Competition acts to keep prices low and service levels high. Competition also encourages innovation. So standards can encourage the development of a varied range of attractive, state-of-the-art products.

Standards also create stability. As a standard becomes established, with the involvement of many suppliers, rapid changes begin to carry high costs and risks. This in turn seeks to protect customer investment.

For all of these reasons it is vital that organisations choose widely adopted standards when making major commitments to information networks, whether these are implemented on a workgroup level or strategically throughout the whole company.

A Review of the OSI Reference Model

In order for computers to communicate with each other they must use a common set of communication protocols at each end of the communications link.

When the International Standards Organisation (ISO) began to develop standards for communications protocols, it started by designing a structure. In order to simplify the specification of the protocols, and create flexibility in their implementation, ISO defined a structure which comprises seven layers. This structure is known as the Open Systems Interconnection (OSI) Reference Model, and is shown in Figure 6 on the following page.

Within this model, each layer provides a specific service. The layers are stacked in a hierarchy, the lowest of which (layer one or the physical layer) defines aspects of the network hardware, such as connection and electrical transmission characteristics.

The highest layer (layer seven or the application layer) defines communications for specific applications, such as file transfer, electronic mail or graphical data exchange. The layers in between specify such aspects as how data is passed over the network, routing over multiple networks, error recovery, dialogue management and data syntax.

It is important to understand that the OSI Reference Model does not itself specify how to implement a communication system: that is the job of the actual protocols. The Reference Model simply provides a structure in which a set of protocols should be specified.

Following the publication of the Reference Model, ISO has gone on to specify actual protocols within each of the seven layers. The early work concentrated on the lower layers, progressing to the higher layers as the lower ones were specified. Indeed there is still much work to do before a complete set of protocols, and particularly the upper layers, will be fully defined.

Layer	Function
7 Application	Special purpose services
6 Presentation	Data formats & representation
5 Session	Dialogue management
4 Transport	Reliable end-to-end data transfer
3 Network	Internetwork routing
2 Data Link	Point-to-point data transfer
1 Physical	Hardware & electrical specifications

Figure 6: The OSI reference model

However, the specification of protocols has not been confined to ISO. The Reference Model has long been accepted by independent LAN and communications vendors, and a number of these have specified their own layered protocols within the structure of the OSI Reference Model. A number of these are now established in the marketplace and have the support of multiple vendors.

Network Hardware Standards

There are now four main hardware standards that will be important for office local area networking over the next ten years:

- Ethernet
- twisted pair Ethernet
- Token Ring
- FDDI

In each case these standards define the physical layer (connection and transmission) and part of the data link layer (topology and media access control). In each case these standards have attracted strong support from a wide range of manufacturers. The key aspects of these standards are listed in Figure 7 overleaf.

Ethernet and twisted pair Ethernet

Ethernet currently offers the highest price/performance, combined with economical and widely available cabling components. Twisted pair Ethernet is a relatively new implementation of Ethernet that is cabled in a star configuration, using active data concentrators at the hub of the star.

Ethernet combines the advantages of high performance, a structured cabling system (AT&T's Premises Distribution System) together with the ability to utilise existing twisted pair phone wiring. Twisted pair Ethernet was finally ratified as a standard by the IEEE 802.3 committee in late 1989, and is backed by AT&T, Olivetti, Hewlett-Packard and Synoptics, amongst others.

Token Ring and FDDI

Token Ring is a network hardware standard developed by IBM. Like twisted pair Ethernet, it too offers the major benefit of a structured cabling system (in this case the IBM Cabling System, based on shielded twisted pair cable). It is available in 4 Mbit/s and 16 Mbit/s versions. Its primary benefit is its support for direct network connections to large IBM host systems.

FDDI is another token passing network topology, but operates at much higher speeds than IBM Token Ring (100 Mbit/s) and runs over fibre optic cables. Because of its relatively high cost, its main area of application is in connecting very high performance workstations, and in implementing high speed network backbone systems to interconnect lower speed local area networks.

Selecting the Right Standards

Any of these standards is suitable for the installation of large office networks, but there are significant variations in cost, performance and ease of cabling. Care must be taken in selecting the most appropriate standard in any given network installation.

Increasingly, network operating system software can support different network hardware types as standards become

	Ethernet	Twisted Pair Ethernet	Token Ring	FDDI
IEEE standard	802.3	802.3 10BaseT	802.5	-
Bandwidth (Mbit/s)	10.0	10.0	4.0 or 16.0	100.0
Topology	Bus	Star	Logical ring, physical star	Logical ring, physical star
Connectivity	PCs, workstations, minicomputers	PCs, workstations, minicomputers	PCs, IBM hosts	PCs, limited range of hosts
Cabling system	Unstructured	Structured (AT&T Premises Distribution System)	Structured (IBM Cabling System)	Structured
Price/performance	High	High	Medium	High performance, high price
Promoters	DEC, Xerox, Intel	AT&T, HP, Synoptics	IBM	AMD, Sun

Figure 7: Key hardware standards for office networks

established for software interfaces between the network adapter, network driver software and network operating software.

Software-based Communications Protocols

The only networking protocols that will endure in the future are those that are endorsed by multiple vendors. These may be official standards that are endorsed by standards bodies such as ISO and IEEE, or they may be de facto standards that have become widely adopted by many vendors. Proprietary protocols that cannot attract multi-vendor support, like languages spoken by only one tribe, will die.

Over recent years, many organisations have specified and introduced networking protocols. Some of these have come and gone through lack of vendor support, and others are clearly on a downward trend.

Of these protocols, there are three protocol sets (sometimes referred to as protocol stacks) which are either stable, with established multi-vendor support, or are continuing to attract support from new vendors. These are:

- IBM protocols
- TCP/IP and related protocols
- ISO protocols

These are depicted in Figure 8 overleaf, and are described in further detail below.

IBM protocols

These are the protocols introduced by IBM for PC to PC communication on Token Ring networks. They do not form

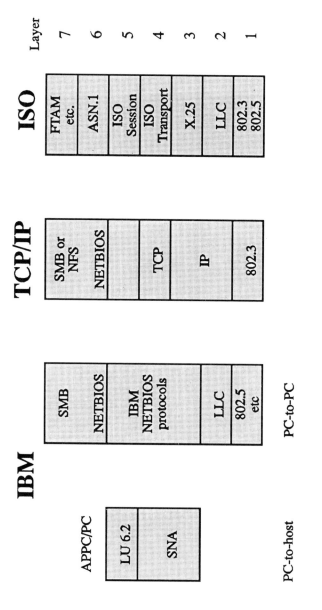

Figure 8: Key software standards for office networks

part of any agreed international standard, but because of the influence of IBM in the marketplace they have become an important de-facto standard.

Protocols for layers two to five are embodied in IBM's LAN Support Program product. At layer two, IBM has adopted the Logical Link Control (LLC) protocol, which also forms part of the ISO protocol set. (The IBM implementation of LLC is a slightly extended version of the ISO LLC specification).

At layers three to five, IBM has adopted a set of proprietary protocols, called NETBEUI protocols, which while sufficient for LAN communication do not provide a very comprehensive layered protocol implementation. Despite this, some products have emerged which provide protocol compatibility with the IBM LAN Support Program at these layers.

The most significant aspect of this product is perhaps not the protocols themselves, but the programming interfaces which IBM has specified to the communication software. IBM provides two important interfaces: NETBIOS, which provides an interface to the session layer, and DLC, which provides an interface to the LLC (the data link layer).

The protocols at layers six and seven are embodied in IBM's PC LAN Program and OS/2 LAN Server. While this does not provide anything like a complete set of layer seven protocols, it does use the Server Message Block (SMB) protocol for communications between workstations, file servers and print servers. This is the same protocol used by Microsoft in its MS Networks and OS/2 LAN Manager products.

In addition to these protocols, IBM has introduced additional protocols for PC-to-host communication. These are used in IBM's APPC/PC product and are based on the LU 6.2 definition within IBM's Systems Network Architecture (SNA).

APPC/PC still relies on LLC at layer two. This enables the two sets of protocols (NETBEUI and LU 6.2) to co-exist within a single network.

TCP/IP and related protocols

TCP/IP is a US Department of Defense protocol which has been widely adopted in the US government, military and educational sectors, and also in the Unix community. TCP/IP was originally designed as a common networking standard for connecting dissimilar devices to wide area networks, but has since been adapted to run on LANs, principally on Ethernet.

TCP/IP protocols cover layers two to four of the OSI Reference Model, and are supported by almost all the Unix vendors. At the higher layers, for workstation to server communication, Sun's NFS (Network File System) has become the dominant protocol standard in the Unix world.

Sun shipped the first implementation of Network File System (NFS) in 1985 for Sun-3 Unix-based workstation systems. NFS was originally designed with the following objectives in mind:

- Machine and operating system independence
- Crash recovery
- Transparent access
- Support for Unix filesystem semantics on Unix client machines
- High performance

At the UniForum Conference in February 1986, 16 different vendor ports of NFS were demonstrated, all sharing files over an Ethernet. From that point, NFS has emerged as the dominant standard for open network systems.

An implementation of NFS for MS-DOS systems, called PC-NFS, was completed by Sun within twelve months of the original Sun-3 version.

The market adopted NFS as the standard largely because it was the only Unix network standard that could offer both a high performance file service, was implemented on standard TCP/IP network protocols, and that could support mixed populations of different machine architectures. Its emergence was helped by Sun's liberal licensing terms, which resulted in NFS source and object code being licensed by over 150 original equipment manufacturers (OEMs).

Indeed, so overwhelming is NFS's dominance in the Unix market that AT&T - the original developers of Unix - now licenses NFS from Sun and ships it with its own range of Unix systems. The great achievement of Sun's NFS and related Open Network Computing (ONC) standards was that they provided a truly comprehensive set of facilities to allow customers to build standardised open network systems using hardware from a variety of vendors. Other networking standards, whether de facto standards or committee standards, have generally failed to deliver a complete set of facilities from the outset, which then results in proprietary workarounds by different applications software developers to fill in the gaps.

The emergence of a NETBIOS interface standard for TCP/IP networks (called RFC 1002) has enabled software originally developed for IBM networks to be implemented on TCP/IP networks. Microsoft's OS/2 LAN Manager software has been ported by Hewlett-Packard to the Unix environment, and this product is known as LAN Manager/X. It operates in conjunction with TCP/IP protocols and the NETBIOS interface, and is promoted by HP as an alternative standard to NFS for file and print service on TCP/IP networks.

ISO protocols

The ISO protocols are the most complete set of local area networking protocols yet specified, in that they cover all seven layers of the OSI Reference Model and provide an extensive set of application layer protocols. However, many of the individual OSI protocols are still evolving, and the number of commercial implementations is limited.

One current drawback with these protocols stems from the fact that OSI is concerned only with the communications aspects, and remains independent of the machine architecture issues surrounding specific implementations. As a result, the software interfaces to the various layers (e.g. for PC-based systems) have yet to be specified.

OSI protocols are now beginning to be implemented in commercial systems. A major stimulus for this has been the need for vendors to conform to common governmental open systems requirements for LAN procurements (as specified by the Government Open Systems Interconnection Profile - GOSIP) in both Europe and North America. However, OSI protocol implementations are bulky, which is a problem for networked PCs where the DOS 640k barrier severely restricts the memory available for networking protocol software.

OSI standards have been more successful in the field of wide area networking. In the UK and Europe, the most widely implemented approach to wide area networking is packet switching, in which chunks of data called packets are given a destination address and sent over the network. The OSI standard for packet switching is called X.25. It defines the communications protocol for wide area networking up to ISO level three, and is also specified in a cut-down form in the ISO local area network protocol stack.

We can expect OSI protocols for local area networking to be incorporated within the ONC/NFS architecture as an alternative to TCP/IP protocols during the next few years.

Other Important Network Protocol Standards

NetWare

Novell's NetWare has, during the 1980s, emerged as the dominant standard for PC local area networking, where PC-compatible hardware is used to provide file and print services. NetWare implements Novell's proprietary IPX protocols at ISO levels two and three, and NetWare Core Protocols (NCP) at the higher levels. NetWare is essentially a specialised file/print server operating system running on IBM PC compatibles, optimised to provide high performance file service. NetWare can operate on a wide variety of network hardware topologies, and can be configured to provide a NETBIOS interface. Many third party gateway products are available for linking PCs connected to NetWare-based networks into a variety of host systems.

NetWare network services have been implemented on VAX minicomputers (NetWare for VMS) and more recently on Unix systems with a product called Portable NetWare. Portable NetWare implements the same IPX and NCP protocols as the standard NetWare product, but runs instead on a Unix-based server.

Its main benefit is the ability to connect existing PC client systems running the NetWare shell client software to Unix multiuser systems and servers. It is likely to be most relevant to companies with large existing investments in Novell networks who wish to introduce Unix-based multiuser systems into their organisation.

Wide Area Networking Protocols

Three important protocol standards have emerged in wide area networking, and it is important to make the right choice between these and other internet working methods when linking networks between remote sites.

SNA

SNA protocols were originally defined by IBM as the standard means of communicating between terminals and IBM mainframe systems. Originally designed for terminal-host communication, they have since been adapted to allow peer-peer communication between PCs. However, SNA networks are generally less efficient and less flexible than TCP/IP or X.25 networks for peer to peer network communication across wide area networks.

For those large organisations that have made major investments in SNA networks as part of their IBM computing infrastructure, it may make sense to use these for LAN to LAN communication. For organisations without established SNA networks, TCP/IP or X.25 will usually be the most cost-effective choice.

TCP/IP

TCP/IP is the most commonly used wide area networking protocol in non-IBM environments in the USA. This protocol is extensively used in US Department of Defence and US academic networks. It is much less commonly used in Europe, where X.25 has a much greater following. However, TCP/IP protocols are now bundled with most vendors' Unix operating systems, so it can be the most cost-effective choice when connecting Unix systems across remote sites.

X.25

The most widely implemented approach to wide area networking in Europe is based on the OSI wide area networking standard, X.25. X.25 defines the communications protocol for wide area networking up to ISO level three, and is also specified in a cut-down form in the OSI local area network protocol stack.

British Telecom and many other PTTs offer public X.25 network services (e.g. BT's PSS), which companies can use for interconnecting their local area networks and other computer systems. Many large organisations have built private X.25 networks for their own internal use.

Within Europe, X.25 is generally the optimal standards choice for building wide area networks, because of its wide support by product vendors and by value added network (VAN) service vendors. X.25 is also the foundation for the X.400 messaging standard, and the emerging EDIFACT electronic data interchange standards. For this reason, X.25-based wide area networks will be able to provide a greater range of network services as these standards gain acceptance.

Both SNA protocols and TCP/IP protocols can be transported over X.25-based wide area networks. The standard method of carrying SNA over X.25 is to use a protocol called QLLC. TCP/IP sessions can be set up across X.25 networks using products called IP routers.

Other Methods of Wide Area Network Interconnection

For some network installations, it may be more appropriate to provide local area network bridges that link LANs at ISO layer two - at the network frame or media access control (MAC) level. In this way wide area links can be provided that are independent of any of the higher level protocols that may be running on the LAN, thus providing greater flexibility of interconnection between sites. So-called MAC-level bridges are widely available for Ethernet-based networks, and are now beginning to appear for Token Ring networks.

Distributed Applications and Interprocess Communications (IPC)

Distributed applications comprise a client-side user interface component, and a server-based component linked across the network by an interprocess communication (IPC) mechanism. Software developers may use a number of different IPC mechanisms to create distributed applications, including NETBIOS, RPC, Named Pipes and IBM's APPC.

Out of these four alternative mechanisms, none has yet emerged as a dominant standard. Each is backed by a different grouping of vendors: NETBIOS is often chosen by independent software vendors because of its network independence; RPC socket interfaces (in a variety of different implementations) are supported by the Unix vendor community; Named Pipes is backed by Microsoft; and APPC is an IBM standard. Because there is no clear single standard, care must be taken at the network design stage to ensure that the IPC requirements of proposed network applications can be supported by the chosen network software protocol stacks. Some IPC mechanisms are quite memory intensive and may restrict the space available for running applications in DOS workstations.

Operating System Standards

Operating system standards need to be considered at two levels: at the client PC or workstation, and at the server. Quite different criteria apply when judging the ability of an operating system to perform the two very different roles of a workstation operating system and a server operating system.

Workstation Operating Systems

DOS

DOS, the single-user, single-tasking operating system developed by Microsoft and backed by IBM, has become the de facto standard for the PC industry over the last eight years. With over 20 million PCs worldwide running PC-DOS (or MS-DOS - the Microsoft variety of DOS), this operating system currently dominates the personal computing landscape. Yet DOS in its current form has many limitations, the following three being perhaps the most significant:

- 640 kbyte memory limit
- lack of a standard user interface environment
- lack of multi-tasking facilities

Despite these limitations, DOS looks like remaining the primary operating system for desktop computers for the next decade. The base of application software, programming tools, device drivers and utility programs that has been developed for DOS-based systems is now so large, and users' commitments to these products so entrenched, that any erosion of DOS's market position will be slow. With the introduction of Windows 3.0, Microsoft has to a greater or lesser degree overcome each of the three major limitations of DOS listed above. This will allow the life of DOS to be extended well beyond its original intended lifespan.

Microsoft Windows

Microsoft Windows is a graphical user interface environment that operates in conjunction with the DOS operating system. Although Windows has been around since the mid-1980s, it was only with the release of Windows 3.0 that it gained significant momentum in the marketplace.

Windows 3.0 can use memory beyond the normal DOS limit of 640 Kbytes in a much more flexible way than previous Windows versions. Applications developed to run within Windows 3.0 all have the same look and feel, and can directly access up to 16 Mbytes of PC memory. Much of Window's popularity derives from its efficient use of machine resources, allowing it to operate on 286 and 386-based systems with only one Mbyte of RAM.

OS/2

IBM's strategic operating system for PCs and workstations for the next decade is OS/2. OS/2 is a totally new operating system co-developed by Microsoft and IBM with the objective of eventually replacing DOS as the standard operating system for IBM-compatible PCs. Originally shipped in November 1987, it has been significantly upgraded during 1988 - 1990. However, to date its market penetration has been low - below five per cent of IBM-compatible users.

OS/2 includes a GUI called Presentation Manager, which is very similar in appearance to MS-Windows. However, OS/2 faces strong competition, not only from the Macintosh Finder and from MS-Windows itself, but increasingly from the Unix operating system. Future versions of OS/2 will be able to run both DOS and Windows applications, and this capability should ensure a continuing and increasing role for this operating system.

Apple MultiFinder

Apple, with their Finder and MultiFinder graphical operating systems for the Macintosh, pioneered the use of the GUI on office desktop computers. MultiFinder is a full multitasking version of the original Finder operating system. Apple have also developed a version of Unix, called A/UX, which can run both Unix and Macintosh application software.

As a result of their early start, the Macintosh computers benefit from the broadest choice of graphical applications in the market today. The Macintosh has retained its lead as the easiest to use and most intuitive desktop system.

Unix

AT&T's long-established Unix operating system is becoming more popular on workstations, starting from an established base in the engineering workstation marketplace. Unix is fast becoming a standard for many government workstation procurement contracts and this alone will ensure that it is a strong contender as a workstation operating system standard. Even IBM has hedged its bets by adopting its own flavour of Unix - AIX - for its range of high-end workstations.

Two different user interface standards are being promoted in the Unix world. Open Look, developed by Sun Microsystems, is backed by the Unix international consortium of manufacturers, led by AT&T. Motif is a competing graphical user interface system backed by the Open Software Foundation (OSF) led by IBM and DEC. Both Open Look and Motif incorporate the X-Windows interface standards developed at the Massachusetts Institute of Technology, so there is some degree of commonality between them.

X-Windows

The X-Window System was the outcome of an MIT project (the Athena project) whose objective was to develop a method of allowing a single graphical application to run on any machine architecture without being rewritten. X-Windows is therefore completely independent of the machine operating system. It is now being promoted as an international standard by a group of manufacturers called the X Consortium, and has been incorporated into most Unix workstation operating systems.

X-Windows is simple in concept, but has been widely misunderstood. It is no more than a protocol that defines the structure of messages between its two components, the client and the server. This two-part structure allows an application program to remain ignorant of the underlying hardware on which it is being displayed, and where it is being displayed.

If a program wishes to draw a line on the screen, or open a window, it requests these services from the X-server program, which then has the task of interfacing to the hardware. Thus, applications are portable between different machine architectures. Since the clients and server communicate via standard communications channels within the operating system, the requests can be sent from one machine to another via a network, permitting the application to be run on one machine, but the user interaction to take place on another.

An X-Windows server generally sits on the local system and the X-Windows client on the remote system - the reverse arrangement to what is normally implied by the term client-server. It is easy to become confused between the meaning of client and server in X-Windows terminology and the meaning of client-server in distributed applications terminology.

X-Windows provides no defined mechanism for moving or resizing windows, no guide as to what windows should look like, and no icons. These facilities are provided by a window manager - to deal with the windows - and a desktop manager - to provide the icons. X-Windows can operate in conjunction with the two principal Unix window manager standards, Open Look and Motif, and has become a standard part of both of these systems.

Making choices

Ultimately, the choice of workstation hardware and workstation operating system should be driven by the variety, quality and suitability of available software applications for end users in the client organisation. Increasingly, the population of different workstation types on networks will become more varied as users migrate to the best operating system for their particular application area. As a result, information networks will need to be designed to be able to accommodate a combination of the four of the key workstation operating system standards. These standards are compared in Figure 9 overleaf.

	DOS	OS/2	Macintosh	Unix
Max. RAM addressable	640 Kb	16 Mb (64 Mb OS/2 V3.0)	16 Mb	Up to memory limit of machine
Graphical user interface	MS Windows	Presentation Manager	Macintosh Finder	Open Look or OSF Motif
CPUs supported	Intel 80X86	Intel 80X86	Motorola 680X0	CPU independent
Minimum practical RAM requirement	512 Kb (DOS) 1 Mb (Windows)	6 Mb	1 Mb	6 Mb
Multitasking?	DOS - no Windows-cooperative	Yes - pre-emptive	Yes - cooperative	Yes - pre-emptive
Multiuser?	No	No	No	Yes
Developer	Microsoft	IBM, Microsoft	Apple	AT&T USO

Figure 9: Key operating system standards for office workstations

Server Operating Systems

The requirements for a server operating system are rather more stringent than for a workstation operating system. A server is a shared system; it must respond rapidly to service requests from many users at once. It must provide the security and data integrity facilities of a minicomputer. The operating system must be able to run multiple services - such as mail, database and communications services, as well as file and print service - without significant performance degradation. In short, the server operating system is a key foundation component of your departmental or central information system.

The main future contenders for a standard server operating system are NetWare/386, OS/2 LAN Manager, and Unix. Each has particular strengths and weaknesses which are presented in Figure 10 overleaf.

The choice of a server operating system should be determined principally by a) the connectivity requirements of the existing workstation population and host systems; and b) scaleability - the capability of the operating system to run on different computer hardware offering a wide range of processing power.

This allows an organisation to expand the processing power of the server without changing the overall network or server operating system architecture. In IBM environments, the connectivity requirements for linking to IBM hosts may increasingly favour OS/2-based servers. In non-IBM or mixed system environments, Unix servers are likely to offer the best combination of connectivity and scaleability. In environments where PCs predominate, and server performance is the overriding objective, then NetWare may be the most appropriate choice.

	OS/2 Lan Manager	Unix/NFS	NetWare
DOS overhead	90-220K	55 - 120K	35K
File/print service	+++	++	++++
Security service	+++	+++	+++
Database service	-(++)	+++	-
Mail service	+	+++	+
Comms service	++	++	--
Task protection	Yes	Yes	No
32-bit support	Coming	Yes	Yes

Figure 10: Server operating system comparison

CHAPTER 7

DATABASES AND INFORMATION NETWORKS

A database is no more than a logical grouping of one or more data files which hold your business information. Business information is collected in a variety of ways e.g. through the recording of business transactions. An effective database management system (DBMS) is needed to ensure that the maximum value is extracted from this information over time. When designing and implementing an information network, the selection of your database system will be one of your most critical and far-reaching decisions.

Relational Database Systems

Most business information naturally has a hierarchical structure; transactions belong to specific accounts, clients belong to sales regions, etc. The first mainframe database management systems organised their data using a hierarchical model, so that the efficiency of processing this hierarchical business data was maximised. The problem with a hierarchical database is that it is difficult to predict in advance what the business data relationships are going to be, and any restructuring of the business almost certainly changes some of these relationships, requiring a restructuring of the database. When databases grow in size from fairly small (e.g. 100 Mbytes) to large (e.g. ten gigabytes) this restructuring task can take several days of elapsed time, time which is simply not available on a production mainframe computer.

The solution to this problem came with the development of the relational database. A relational database stores data in tables, each of which is called a relation and which contains a number of records and fields. Unlike a hierarchical database, a relational database imposes very little structure on the data when it is stored; instead of permanent linkages among items a relational database allows temporary relationships to be established by query commands. This allows file manipulations, e.g. extractions and joins, to be done easily and permits powerful, efficient query languages to be developed.

The mathematician E. F. Codd has defined twelve Fidelity Rules that clarify the features of a true relational database model. Many database products claim to be relational, but only a small proportion actually meet all of Codd's rules.

Structured Query Language

The only concrete expression of the relational model that has won broad industry acceptance is IBM's Structured Query Language, or SQL. Four different dialects of SQL have been incorporated into IBM's DBMS products: DB2 (MVS), SQL/DS (VM), SQL/400 (AS/400) and Database Manager (OS/2 EE). Subsequently, SQL has been adopted as a standard by four important standards bodies: ANSI, ISO, the Open Software Foundation and by X/Open.

SQL is a language for interacting with relational databases, but is not an application development language. SQL statements must be embedded in conventional programming languages and preprocessed to translate the SQL calls into optimised database calls specific to the host computer language.

The increasing popularity of the SQL database standard has major benefits for business users in providing a standard software query interface to database systems. This potentially allows vendors to develop a wide variety of SQL database query tools that can be used with a range of different SQL database products.

The Importance of Getting On-line

The traditional backroom, batch approach to computer processing is being rapidly replaced by the use of front-office, transaction-based decision support and record-keeping tools operating in an on-line mode. The banking, financial services, manufacturing and communications industries have set the pace in the implementation of on-line systems to date. However, participants in all major business and public sector markets are experimenting with on-line systems in an effort to provide their organisations with more timely information.

Within Europe, the trends leading to the creation of a unified European market ('1992') are leading organisations to increase their investment in on-line systems, in response to a more competitive business environment.

Certain types of business information such as financial accounts are by definition status reports at a point in time. It does not matter if the records are updated continuously or in batches. However, in the mainstream business operating functions it matters a great deal if records are not updated continuously as changes occur. A stock file is of no use to a warehouse manager if it doesn't tell you what is in stock today.

Business information only has value if it can tell management at a glance what it really needs to know. Batch systems may produce reams of printed data that simply obscure the vital things that managers need to know, because the numbers they show are out of date.

On-line transaction processing

An on-line database management system will manage business data in real time, so that the contents of the databases reflect the actual status of the business and its transaction history at any given moment. The computer processing of business transactions in real time is called on-line transaction processing, or OLTP.

Initially, OLTP applications were run on mainframes, and mainframes are still the OLTP workhorse in environments where high transaction rates, above 100 transactions per second (tps), need to be handled. However, during the 1980s much of the innovation in OLTP was driven by minicomputer vendors. Minicomputers, which are optimised for the processing of events as they occur, are ideal partners for OLTP. The minicomputer OLTP market is dominated by the OLTP specialists Tandem and Stratus. Other market participants include the general purpose minicomputer vendors such as DEC and the Unix supermini vendors such as Pyramid and Sequent. Mini-OLTP systems address the mid-range transaction processing market, for transaction rates between 20 and 200 tps.

The third market tier of micro-based OLTP systems has been created by the availability of powerful 32-bit workstations and network servers. Software to harness these computers for OLTP is now becoming available, and micro-based OLTP is likely to grow rapidly as the most cost-effective solution for transaction processing in departments and in small/medium sized companies, for transaction rates between five and 50 tps.

SQL database systems that are optimised for OLTP applications must include a number of specialised features. The software must guard against corruption of the database if the computer stops for any reason during the processing of a transaction. A mechanism called two-phase commit is often used to ensure that transactions are unambiguously entered into the database, and transaction rollback facilities are provided so that the system administrator can 'rewind' the system back through its transaction history to reach a convenient restart point in the event of system failure.

Examples of SQL DBMS products optimised for transaction processing include IBM's DB2 for IBM mainframes, and the portable OLTP databases - including Oracle, Ingres and Sybase - which have been implemented on a range of mini and micro-based systems.

Implementing Databases on Networks

The development of relational databases, and in particular the standardisation of SQL, has made possible today's generation of networked client-server database systems.

At the most basic level, databases can be networked by providing terminal emulation facilities on PC workstations that connect through to the database host. In this way, a central database can be made accessible to network users both from the local site and from remote sites across wide area network links. With this approach, all of the database processing is being performed by the host computer, and the network is being used simply as a means of transferring terminal screen and keyboard data between the host and the user.

The first multiuser PC databases were a straightforward adaptation of simple single-user PC DBMS products. PCs on the network accessed database files residing on the file server, which was used as a shared hard disk. In these multiuser file-sharing databases, all database processing is performed by the database software in the PCs.

Benefits of client-server databases systems

Over the last few years, client-server database systems have been developed, where the database processing is split between a user interface client application running on the workstation and a database server application running on the host computer or network server. The client-server DBMS combines the benefits of both the host-based and multiuser file-sharing DBMS approaches, and avoids the inherent drawbacks in either.

A client-server database handles user input via its user interface client component, and passes high level database requests over the network to the database server. Because these requests are at a high level, the network traffic generated is correspondingly low. In contrast, a multiuser file-sharing database has to open the database files on the file server, pass the database index information over the network to the workstation, and locate the database record by searching across the network through the portion of the database specified by the index. All of this involves sending a large quantity of data over the network to be processed in the client workstation. As the number of workstations on the network increases, a data bottleneck is soon reached due to the limited bandwidth of the network connection to the file server. This severely limits the number of concurrent users on such a system.

A client-server system generates much less traffic on the network. The bottleneck is no longer the network connection, but simply the capacity of the database server to process the database requests. Because these requests are processed within a single computer, there is a much higher bandwidth between the server processor and the hard disks on which the database files reside, with the result that many more user requests can generally be serviced before the response time degrades to an unacceptable level. Client-server databases should even outperform host-based databases because there is no need for the host to process user interface operations.

The lower network traffic levels generated by terminal-host and client-server database systems have another important user benefit: they allow databases to be accessed from users on remote sites, over wide area links which have more limited bandwidth, typically between 1200 bps and 64 kbps. In contrast, the use of multiuser file-sharing databases is generally restricted to a single site.

Terminal-host and client-server database systems have far superior data integrity and security properties compared to a multiuser file-sharing DBMS. Central host or server-based security mechanisms can be enforced at the database level rather than only at the file level. Transaction tracking and rollback facilities can be implemented in a way that is not possible with the multiuser file-sharing approach.

The multiuser file-sharing DBMS, together with the single-user PC DBMS from which it is derived, takes advantage of the local processing capabilities of the PC to implement a user interface which is generally superior to that of a host-based DBMS. A client-server DBMS shares this advantage, and vendors are beginning to implement client database front-ends using graphics user interface environments such as MS-Windows and X-Windows.

A key requirement of client-server database systems is a mechanism for interprocess communication (IPC) between the client program and the database server program. Different IPC mechanisms are required by different client-server database products, and these mechanisms are not all supported by some types of networking software.

The advantages and disadvantages of the different network database architectures are summarised in Figure 11.

Database type	Multiuser host-based	Multiuser file-sharing	Multiuser client-server
Host processing?	Yes	No	Yes
Workstation processing?	No - only terminal emulation	Yes	Yes
Network traffic?	Low	High	Low
Data security & integrity	High	Low	High
Database performance?	High, degrades slowly	OK for small no. of users, but degrades rapidly	High, degrades slowly

Figure 11: Pros and cons of network database architectures

The Need for Fault Tolerance in On-line Systems

All computer systems fail eventually. In a batch environment, failures can be frequently recovered without significant disruption to the business by restarting the batch job. When an OLTP system fails, the entire business can grind to a halt, since backup paper-based systems fall rapidly into disuse after the introduction of computer-based transaction record-keeping.

Fault-tolerance is not an absolute concept. There are different levels of fault-tolerance that can be implemented within a computer system, depending upon the reliability requirements of the organisation, and the price it is willing to pay for that level of reliability. When considering the technical aspects of fault-tolerance, it is worth considering the principal causes of failure in computer systems:

Factors contributing to systems failures

Tandem Computers have reported on the different factors contributing to system failure in minicomputers:

- Administrative errors   45 per cent
- Software errors   25 per cent
- Unknown causes   13 per cent
- Power failure   9 per cent
- Disk failure   7 per cent
- Processor failure   1 per cent

Source: *Tandem Technical Report*, June 1985

An information network is a more complex system than a minicomputer linked to terminals. In a business information network, a critical failure is a system component failure that affects more than one user of the system. In networks, as in minicomputers, it is safe to assume that administrative errors and software errors will predominate. However, critical failures on networks can arise not only from a failure in the shared processing resources - the servers - but also from failures in the network cabling system itself. There is also the possibility of the failure of a workstation or the workstation network adapter, but this will not generally be a catastrophic failure because it will generally affect only a single user. That user can usually move relatively painlessly to another workstation if a failure occurs.

According to a survey conducted in 1987 by First Market Research, the single most important factor influencing decisions to purchase PC-based networks was reliability. Over 93 per cent of respondents rated reliability as either 'very important' or 'of critical importance' to their purchase decision.

Levels of protection

When we consider fault-tolerance in a network environment, the following levels of protection against system failure can be defined:

Level I: protection against server disk media failure

Level II: protection as level I, plus protection against disk or disk controller failure

Level III: protection as level II, plus protection against processor, power supply or any other server failure

Level IV: protection as level III, plus protection against any network cabling system or transceiver failure

Level V: protection as level IV, plus protection against any hardware failure in the entire network system, including any hardware failure in a workstation

Level I fault tolerance is achieved by server operating system facilities that provide read after write verification and 'hot-fixing' of disk media defects. Level II is achieved by server disk mirroring. Level III can be achieved by duplexing a pair of servers, with each server monitoring the activity of the other and being able to take over in the event of a server malfunction. Level IV fault tolerance requires duplexed cabling systems, where individual workstations are connected to servers by two network cabling systems. If there is a cable break in one system, the workstation switches over to the alternative cabling system, either automatically or by manual intervention by the network administrator. Level V fault-tolerance requires specialised fault-tolerant workstations.

On-line information network systems in business environments are likely to need fault tolerant capabilities only up to level IV. Level V fault tolerance will be very expensive (requiring at least four times the investment in workstation hardware) and is likely to be restricted to military environments for the foreseeable future.

Fault-tolerant capabilities at levels III and IV are only just becoming available in the network marketplace. However, fault-tolerant capabilities at levels I and II have been available for network servers for some time, and add a price premium of only 20 to 30 per cent to the total system. For business environments, this additional cost can almost always be cost-justified by the increased system availability that results.

At a minimum, all network servers should be protected from power supply failure by the provision of an uninterruptible power supply (UPS). UPS systems are available for between £500 and £1,000 per server.

The Concept of the Information Repository

In addition to the costs of buying and running a DBMS, much time and effort is expended by organisations in entering business information into its databases. If all this expenditure is not to be wasted, it is vital that information can be retrieved from the database easily by users in a format that can assist them in making business decisions.

Information networks in the future will be designed around the concept of a common repository of business information, structured as a relational SQL DBMS. As the term repository implies, there is a need to contain and protect a resource which is of very high intrinsic value to the organisation. In addition, easy and flexible access must be provided to the business information database for a variety of user applications, not all of which may have been thought about when the system was first designed.

Getting a common source of business data

A major obstacle to the more effective use of networks has been created by the inability to access a common source of business data from different software application packages. There is valuable information contained within the records of business transactions that must be analysed and presented to senior management to allow them to make effective decisions on the running of the business. An efficient linkage must be constructed between the repository of key business information, and the decision support system (DSS) which may include tools such as spreadsheets and statistical analysis packages. In addition, similar links may be required between the information repository and the network communications facilities, so that central records of business messages can be kept and tracked for later reference. This concept of the common repository of business information is illustrated in Figure 12.

If these links can be provided in a way that minimises the effort required to extract the necessary data, then the value that can be extracted from the business database is multiplied. For example, the business transaction records contain up-to-date information on which customers are active, and which customers are buying specific products. If the information repository concept is properly implemented, the system should allow users in the sales department to identify a particular customer group and transfer name and address information to a word processing package which would then generate a customer mailshot.

SQL provides a standardised way of querying a database that will make this kind of operation possible. Some end-user application tools today, particularly spreadsheet applications such as Lotus 1-2-3 and Microsoft Excel, can now be set up to execute SQL commands and display the resulting information in a way that can be easily tailored by the user.

Reports in real time

An additional key requirement will be to use decision support tools to generate reports from the DBMS in real time. Information used in decision support has much greater value

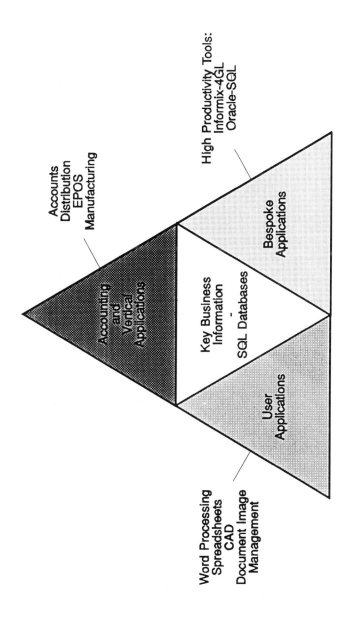

Figure 12: The common repository of business information

if it is absolutely current. Many SQL DBMS products do not permit database query operations while the database is on-line and being updated. Instead, reports must be compiled from the database during inactive periods, e.g. during the night, or a snapshot copy of the database taken which soon becomes outdated. Ideally, the DBMS should be able to support query operations while it is processing transactions, so that a dynamic, on-line view of the required business information can be achieved.

Client-server SQL DBMS products are now beginning to appear on the market that have these capabilities. The client software on the workstation can extract the required information from the database server in real time by passing the appropriate SQL commands over the network, and can then process this information into whatever presentation format is required.

The benefits of this are clear. Instead of management having to make do with monthly, or even weekly status reports of business operations, they will be able to summon up a graphical display of the actual status of the business at that moment in time. This will be structured according to user-selected parameters such as sales of individual product lines by location, and will provide a dynamic 'window on the business' for middle and senior management.

4GLs and CASE Tools - The Step Forward

The complexity of writing database applications

One of the biggest problems in corporate information systems today is how to manage the complexity of writing database applications that handle the processes of database construction, and of data input and query by users. Blueprints for integrated mainframe-based information systems that were laid down in the 1960s have developed into millions of lines of computer code, even in single enterprises. This software is arranged in hundreds of modules, each of which may contain between one and four thousand lines of instructions. Unfortunately much of this code will be poorly structured and therefore incomprehensible even to software experts. Typically the original author will have already moved on, to another department or to another company.

The advent of relational DBMSes, designed to be more easily restructured after the system had been implemented, was supposed to fix this problem. Unfortunately, large mainframe relational database systems have proved to be anything but flexible in practice. The demand for new database applications from end-users has overwhelmed DP departments, whose software engineering methods and tools have not been adequate to keep pace with this demand. The move towards network computing was the first key step to resolving this problem.

Network computing moves the responsibility for creating and maintaining the businesses' databases directly to departments or divisions, so easing the backlog on the central DP department.

The development of so-called fourth generation languages (4GLs) is another key step. 4GLs are very high-level computer languages that are non-procedural, in that they describe what processing is to be done without specifying the particular procedures to be used to complete the processing. 4GLs are the computer languages of the future, because they simplify programming, increase a programmer's productivity, are relatively easy to modify and maintain, and can be understood by a much broader group of people.

Coupled with 4GLs, computer-aided systems engineering (CASE) techniques are now making it possible to generate database application code directly from graphical, high level specifications of how information flows in a business operation. At the heart of a CASE system is a CASE dictionary. This is a special database that contains all the information needed to construct a database system. It supports particular business modelling techniques and validates the consistency and integrity of all information entered into it. Finally, it organises and cross-references the logical, physical and enterprise design of the application. Business terminology is precisely defined in a thesaurus to eliminate misunderstandings of the terms and expressions used in the particular business.

Integrated CASE tool

An integrated CASE tool (I-CASE) combines a front-end CASE tool for generating functional and data diagrams, together with a tightly integrated back-end 4GL code generator. I-CASE tools may be based on either character or graphics user interfaces, but the objective is the same; to link the formal analysis and descriptive phase of generating an application with the code-writing phase in a single integrated system that is extensively automated. I-CASE systems, like any software engineering tools, have related costs. As well as the up-front financial and training investment in the tools, the code that is generated will often run slower than hand-written code and may thus require a more powerful computer processor. However, the benefits of the I-CASE approach, in terms of productivity of applications writing, and superior maintainability of applications code, generally far outweigh the costs. The larger the database project, the more pronounced these benefits will be.

The Need for Standards in Database Development

Integrating CASE tools

As has already been discussed, the central problem for DP and MIS manager today is the ever-increasing percentage of the available program development resource that is being consumed by application software maintenance, leaving less and less available for new application development. To address this problem, a number of different types of software engineering tools have been developed, including compilers, source code maintenance and release control systems, library managers, data dictionaries and panel editors.

However, there is no CASE vendor today that can offer a total CASE solution, that covers the entire software development cycle, from systems requirements, systems analysis, code and data generation, through to debugging and maintenance. Standard methodologies are urgently required to establish ground rules for symbolising diagrammatic representations, for isolating and relating code and data specifications, and for project control of the overall development cycle. Existing methodologies (e.g. SSADM developed by LBMS and the CCTA for systems analysis and code generation) address only part of the development cycle.

There are CASE products currently available to cover all the phases of the development cycle, but unfortunately they have generally been developed in isolation by different vendors. As a result there is significant functional overlap between different products, and integration of these tools into an overall CASE solution is both expensive and time-consuming.

Because of the significant up-front training investment required with CASE, and the accumulation over time of an even greater investment in the lines of database code tied to particular CASE tools, CASE product selection decisions are very expensive to undo.

If the total CASE concept is to succeed, then CASE tools must be provided for each stage of the applications development process that can be coupled together into an integrated whole. To achieve this, standard specifications must be established for the interchange of data definitions. A central information dictionary must be maintained that includes details of security, system configurations, code modules as well as data definitions, acting as a single controlled source of all system information. Such a standard should be an open framework that would force suppliers of CASE tools for one phase to obey the rules for accepting and generating information for other tools in other phases.

AD/Cycle

The first attempt to provide such an overall applications development framework is embodied in IBM's announcement of AD/Cycle. AD/Cycle tools and tool services, provided through both IBM and third parties, will be integrated across all phases of the application development life cycle. AD/Cycle adheres to the SAA Common User Access standards, and will allow the production of SAA-compliant applications.

A key element of AD/Cycle is a database repository built around IBM's DB2 to provide the necessary single point of reference and control for shared application development information.

IBM AD/Cycle products include:

- IBM Repository Manager - providing repository services under the IBM MVS operating system

- DevelopMate modelling tool - which defines a business's processes and data in terms of entity relationship models

- Software Analysis Test Tool - a tool allowing earlier detection of software errors which can graphically depict testing coverage and progress

- Workstation Interactive Test Tool - providing the capability to automatically record and replay interactive application test sessions

- Dictionary Model Transformer - allowing data in existing IBM data dictionaries to be moved to the Repository Manager

AD/Cycle is likely to play a strong future role as a unifying standard for applications development in organisations. We can expect to see products emerge that conform to AD/Cycle and support the development of client-server database applications as well as traditional database systems.

Many database and CASE vendors have pledged that they will follow IBM's AD/Cycle standard. Others may respond to IBM by working together to devise an alternative open standard, or they may attempt to develop their own individual integrated package of tools that can cover the entire applications development cycle.

An open approach such as AD/Cycle will attract a wide variety of compatible third party products and is likely to give greater choice and flexibility to the customer.

Making the Right Database Decisions

Reversing the trend of centralisation

Organisations are more and more attracted by the idea of reversing the process of centralisation of databases on mainframe computers, which dominated DP thinking in the 1960s and 1970s. While expenditures on centralised DBMS systems have mushroomed, the promised benefits from these mainframe-based system have been slow to arrive. Pressure has long been growing to find ways of reducing dependence on mainframe-based DBMSes. Yet there are numerous organisational obstacles to be cleared before client-server DBMS systems can displace the older technologies.

The legacy of mainframe system maintenance is an inescapable fact of life in most large companies. Existing CASE tools speed the delivery of new programs but do little to help with maintaining existing database applications. DP managers have become bogged down in their own internal politics, facing pressure from their own staff and from mainframe vendors to perpetuate the traditional approach.

Despite these obstacles, the first signs of a reversal in the trend towards centralisation became apparent in the 1980s as corporate organisations began to pioneer commercial transaction processing on minicomputer systems. At the beginning of the 1990s we are now seeing the first client-server network DBMSs implemented as live commercial systems.

Safeguarding the information network database

The information contained in your information network databases lies at the core of your business activities. It must be safeguarded as one of your most precious corporate assets.

In OLTP environments, if the database is irreparably damaged for any reason chaos will result. The information in the database must be up-to-date, or it will simply mislead management. And if the information cannot be accessed easily and in a flexible fashion, most of its potential value to your business will be lost.

The DBMS, together with the hardware on which it runs, will account for a significant proportion of the total investment in your information network. The cost lies not only in the system purchase, but in the cost of time spent analysing and creating the different database application programs that allow your business to profit from the business information you own. The specification and implementation of a DBMS is, like the information network of which it is such a key part, a strategic decision for the organisation - one that can have a major impact on the performance of the business.

The product selection process must involve not only the selection of the DBMS itself, but also the selection of a 4GL, a report generator and CASE tools. In addition, you must ensure that your local and wide area networks are able to properly support end-to-end communication between the database users and the database server. Choosing a DBMS without considering these vital related components will reduce your future system flexibility and expansion capability. Even if not acquired at the same time, these products should be evaluated together with the DBMS as a single integrated system.

In an operational business environment, changing to another DBMS vendor is rather like changing the tyres on a car in motion. Together with the selection of your network cabling system and networking software, your network database decisions are the most important you will make, and the most expensive to rectify if you get them wrong.

CHAPTER 8

IMPLEMENTING INTEGRATED NETWORK SYSTEMS

The Need for Integrated Networks

Most businesses today have made significant investments in computer systems of one form or another. These installed systems are based on a variety of different technologies, each of which have little inherent compatibility with each other.

They include:

- Standalone personal computers and workstations used to automate tasks performed by individuals (based on three alternative architectures: IBM PC, Apple Mac or Unix)

- PC local area networks - again, implemented in both large and small organisations, usually at a departmental level

- Supermicros - powerful multiuser systems based on microcomputer technology which are beginning to replace minicomputers

- Minicomputers - implemented in both large and small organisations at a departmental level

- Mainframes - implemented in large organisations at an enterprise level

In most larger organisations, it is likely that the installed systems are composed of a mix of these architectures, each usually implemented in a self-contained fashion and not able to communicate with the others.

The biggest challenge confronting system managers in the 1990s is how to connect together these incompatible and isolated 'islands' of business automation into integrated business-wide information systems.

The penalties of standalone, incompatible systems are high, and include:

- Lack of communication between departments due to inherent problems of information transfer between dissimilar computer systems

- Inaccurate, inconsistent and duplicated business information resulting from fragmented information databases held on multiple systems

- Difficulties in consolidating business information held in incompatible systems

- Inefficiencies introduced by duplicate data entry and the rekeying of information into different systems

- High people costs incurred in maintaining a variety of systems of different architectures, each of which requires its own set of technical skills

System managers need to extricate themselves from this potential chaos, and move towards better integrated computer environments. The only practical and effective way to achieve this is to connect systems together into an integrated network based on an underlying framework of communication standards.

The technology of integration

In the past, there have been vigorous debates between industry pundits about which types of computer technology are most suitable for which commercial applications. To a large degree these arguments are becoming less relevant. Most organisations face the reality of a mix of PCs, some form of multiuser departmental system, some PC networks, and in large organisations a mainframe system.

In the short term, applications are generally tied to a particular hardware technology. The more important argument is thus not 'can I run my business on any one of these technologies' but 'how do I integrate what I have into an integrated computer environment that can deliver business results?'

In particular, there is an ongoing debate about whether PC networks are a more appropriate technology than multi-user systems for departmental computing. Those in favour of PC networking point to the crucial need for desktop computing power to support the new generation of easy-to-use graphical applications. Those in favour of multi-user systems point to the limitations of today's PC network servers in supporting serious multi-user applications.

The arguments are now becoming obsolete. PC networks *and* multi-user systems are here to stay. They can be integrated together in two different ways:

- Existing multi-user systems, whether they are propriety minicomputers or Unix-based supermicros, can be directly connected to PC local area networks, providing PC users with access to both applications running on the multiuser system, and PC applications running across the network.

- Many multiuser systems can now provide a range of PC network services, in addition to running multiuser applications, e.g. DEC's VAX systems can provide file and print sharing for PCs using a product called PCSA. Sun SPARC Unix servers can provide equivalent facilities using PC-NFS.

In this way, a single box can combine the facilities of a multi-user system and a PC LAN server.

Integration is now the key issue, and the arguments have moved on. The key issue for system managers in the 1990s is not 'do I implement LANs or multiuser system?' but 'how can I successfully implement integrated network system?'

If you wish to implement networks that will be successful in achieving your business goals, there are four main issues that need to be considered before you start:

- network architecture and standards support
- reliability and manageability
- ease of use
- scaleability of systems

The logistical and technical challenges of implementing business networks increase with the size of the network. The larger your planned network, the more critical it is that the key issues are well understood in advance.

Network Architecture and Standards Support

When implementing a network that goes beyond a single workgroup, it is vital to design the network around a consistent architecture. A comprehensive architecture will define the key network services and communications standards to be implemented on the network, in the following areas:

- Messaging
- File transfer services
- File and print services

- Terminal services
- Database access and database development
- Directory services
- Security services

If these services can be provided in a standardised way across the entire network or internetwork, then the challenges of system interconnection and network management will be much reduced. Or, to put it another way, if there is no attempt to standardise these services, it will be extremely difficult to achieve a well- integrated network environment, and it will be extremely difficult (and resource-intensive) to manage that environment. Only if a well-integrated business-wide network can be built will the full business benefits be delivered.

Building a network for the long term

The objective of a network architecture then is to provide the necessary framework around which a well-integrated and manageable network can be built. In the same way that architectural plans are required to build a house that will not fall down within its defined lifespan, a network architecture is vital to implementing a durable and resilient business network.

If you are implementing a purely departmental network, architecture considerations may seem less important - in the short term. Don't forget that you may need to link that network into a wider network system in the future. Many networks today have been installed without any consideration of network architecture issues, and organisations are now facing the consequences.

System managers need to establish a network architecture which fits in with the following business constraints:

- Today's short term business requirements
- The longer term business strategy
- The existing investments in computer systems

The methodology used by Ives & Company to define network architectures for individual clients is shown in Figure 13 overleaf. A comprehensive network architecture will specify standard ways of providing key network services. These include the following:

Messaging services

The network architecture should define how electronic mail messages (together with document and binary file enclosures) should be passed between different systems attached to the network.

In an open network environment, the two main alternative standards for messaging are Unix Mail and X.400. X.400 is the OSI standard for messaging.

File transfer services

In any network, data files will need to be transferred between both computers of similar architecture (e.g. PC to PC) and different architectures (e.g. PC to mini). The file transfer standards in the Unix world are UUCP - Unix to Unix Copy Protocol and FTP - File Transfer Protocol. The defined OSI file transfer standard is FTAM, which is being implemented across a range of different machine architectures.

File and print services

All networks provide some type of transparent access to remote disk storage, and remote printing facilities. This is one

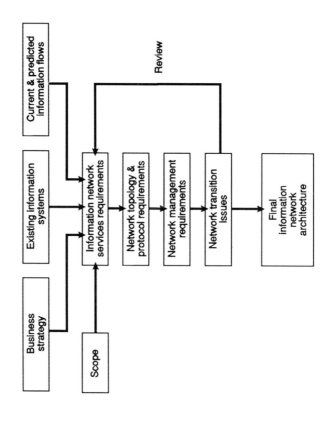

Figure 13: Ives & Company methodology for the definition of network architecture

of the most frequently used network services, and it is important to provide file and print service in a consistent way across the network. In the open systems world, NFS has emerged as the dominant standard.

Terminal services

Together with file/print services, terminal services are the most commonly used network services in most business environments. Terminal services provide the ability to connect into a host across a network as a virtual terminal, which is typically a terminal emulation running on a PC or a workstation.

Directory services

Network directory services are necessary to keep track of user and machine names, addresses and passwords on local and wide area networks. This is an obvious area where it is vital to achieve standardisation across the entire network.

Within the open network computing world, the dominant directory service standard is Sun's YP (Yellow Pages). In the open systems world, the defined standard is X.500, though few products are available that implement it.

Security services

Host computer security levels are defined in a US Department of Defense publication called the *Orange Book*. Security levels are defined according to an A, B, C and D coding scheme. A is the highest level of security, D the least. There are additional sub-categories within each of these levels, e.g. C1, C2.

Within a large network, different security levels will be appropriate for categories of business data. Third party products are available for a number of different host computer architectures, including Unix systems, that provide enhanced levels of security.

Database access and database development

With the increasing amount of business data now held in relational databases, it is becoming more and more important to standardise database management systems across the organisations. This can be achieved at three possible levels: the database query level, the database server level and the database 4GL level.

The most commonly implemented database query standard in the commercial world is IBM's SQL. However, standardising on SQL does not necessarily make it easy to transfer data between database systems. To achieve this, it is necessary to standardise on a specific vendor's database management software.

There are strong arguments for standardising your choice of 4GL development environment across your organisation, not least because it allows you to focus your internal development skills and resources in one skill area. It also provides for maximum simplicity in manipulating and transferring data held in different databases.

Reliability

Unless a network is intrinsically reliable, the promised business benefits will never be achieved. The larger the network, the higher the costs of downtime, because of the wider scale of impact of any single failure event.

The Yankee Group have made the following estimates for system downtime costs in 250 US corporations.

Up to $1,000+ per hour	42 per cent
Up to $10,000 per hour	26 per cent
Up to $50,000 per hour	5 per cent
Over $50,000 per hour	4 per cent
Unknown	23 per cent

Estimated System Downtime Costs -
250 US Corporations - Yankee Group

Depending on the particular site, the costs of downtime can clearly be very high indeed. This is particularly true of so-called 'mission-critical' applications where the business depends upon the reliable operation of key on-line transaction systems.

Departmental network systems rarely run mission-critical applications. These are most often associated with larger-scale, site-wide or business-wide networking installations.

There are four specific measures that can be taken at the network design stage to ensure maximum reliability and uptime of the network:

- Structured cabling system design
- Fault tolerant server configurations
- Server power protection
- Provision of network monitoring and diagnostic facilities

Structured cabling system design

Perhaps the greatest source of network problems is an unreliable cabling system. Simple linear bus networks implemented on thin or thick Ethernet are intrinsically unreliable network topologies. A single point of failure anywhere on the cable can disable the entire network. Unfortunately, such networks have been widely implemented because they are cheap to install, requiring no wiring hubs and relatively little cable. The price to be paid is hours of expensive troubleshooting and debugging time when problems occur.

For any network larger than 20 active nodes, it is advisable to implement a so-called structured cabling system, based on a star-wired topology. Token Ring networks are always implemented in a structured fashion using the IBM cabling system or unshielded twisted pairs. Ethernet networks can be star-wired on either unshielded twisted-pair, shielded twisted-pair or fibre optic cable types. The IEEE standard for implementing Ethernet on unshielded twisted pair (UTP) is 802.3 10BaseT. The current de-facto standard for Ethernet-based fibre optic networks is called FIORL (fibre optic inter-repeater link), with an IEEE standard 802.3 10BaseF in draft form.

Structured Ethernet cabling systems incorporate active electronic hubs called concentrators. If an individual link between a hub and a workstation fails, the rest of the network will continue to operate. For greater levels of fault-tolerance, a structured cabling system can be designed with backup hubs, so that if any single hub fails, the network can recover and use an alternative data path. In addition to offering superior reliability, structured cabling incurs much lower cable reconfiguration costs during staff and office moves.

Fault tolerant server configurations

The network server, being a shared resource, is a critical point of potential network failure. The reliability of network servers can be improved by implementing one or more of the following measures:

- Disk mirroring - where disk reads and writes are duplicated to separate physical disks

- Server mirroring - where database reads and writes are duplicated to two separate servers using a process known as dual-phase commit. This is now supported by a number of SQL DBMS products

- Specialised fault tolerant server technology - using specialised fault-tolerant machine architectures from vendors such as Tandem and Stratus. Recently, both vendors have introduced fault-tolerant Unix server products

Server power protection

The loss of power to a network server will result in lengthy delays before file systems can be rebuilt and the server brought back on-line. In some cases, file system damage may be caused which can only be repaired by restoring data from the last back-up.

These problems can be prevented by installing uninterruptible power supply (UPS) systems. These cost between £600 and £1,000 for a typical departmental server, more for a larger host system. We strongly recommend that all server installations are protected with UPS systems.

Provision of network monitoring and diagnostic facilities

In an operational network environment, pro-active network management is essential so that problems can be identified and fixed before they turn into catastrophic network failures. This can only be achieved by implementing appropriate network monitoring and diagnostic facilities, so that network statistics can be gathered and analysed at a central network management console. These provide valuable testing and troubleshooting aids, reducing the time taken to identify and fix problems.

Commercial network management products available today generally support one of two key standards in network management: SNMP (simple network management protocol - the network management standard for TCP/IP based networks) and NetView (IBM's network management system). Products that implement the OSI network management standards will soon be reaching the market.

To assist very large network installations which are forced to implement more than one management system, we can expect to see network management products that span all three network management worlds: SNMP, NetView and OSI.

Ease of Use

As more and more office workers are linked to information networks, a greater diversity of users will need to gain access to the facilities of the network. These will include many non-technical user groups, including secretaries, middle and senior managers, together with professional and administrative staff. This greater user participation on the network is creating the demand for networks that are much easier to use, and that can provide facilities accessible to anyone in the organisation.

Graphical user interface

If applications can be designed each with the same look and feel, the time taken for users to master new applications and facilities will be much reduced. Following initial research at Xerox's PARC research centre, Apple were the first company to make a commercial success of graphical user interface (GUI) technology, with their Macintosh operating environment. Market research indicates that the average Apple user is proficient in four to five different software applications, compared to one to two in the IBM PC world. A common graphical interface as provided by the Macintosh not only makes it faster to learn and use new applications, but reduces training costs.

IBM have defined standards for character and graphics user interfaces under their Common User Access conventions within their overall systems architecture framework, called SAA. Microsoft's MS-Windows, IBM's OS/2 Presentation Manager and OSF's Motif all adhere to the standard CUA definitions, and as a result all three have a similar look and feel.

Integrated network front-ends or desktop managers are becoming available that present the facilities of the network in a graphical, intuitive way. IBM's OfficeVision is an example of an integrated networked office desktop implemented under a standard GUI - Presentation Manager. Other systems include Microsoft's Windows V3.0 desktop, Hewlett-Packard's New Wave (soon to be available across MS-Windows, OS/2 PM and OSF Motif environments) and IXI's X.desktop (available on a range of Motif-based Unix systems).

The hidden costs of training and end user support are considerably greater than the up-front acquisition costs of the hardware or software. Recent research in the US has shown that between three and five times as much is spent on software training as on the software itself during the lifetime of use of a typical business application package. Applications based on standard graphical interfaces require approximately one half the training and support time compared to conventional character-based applications. For this reason, there are compelling reasons to incorporate graphical user interface standards into the overall architecture of an information network.

Computer-assisted instruction (CAI) and training tools, often built into the application, can make a major contribution to reducing training and support costs. A good CAI system will provide an on-line interactive tutorial on a PC that a user can work with at his or her own speed, which will enable him or her to rapidly learn the basic facilities of an application package.

When upgrading an existing system, there is a tradeoff to make in moving to new graphical applications that can offer the above-mentioned benefits. In some cases, if staff turnover is low and users are satisfied with existing facilities, sticking with older applications may provide a lower cost solution which avoids the need to retrain users.

Scaleability of Systems

Scaleability can be defined as the ability of a system to be scaled up to support a greater number of users, without significant redesign or reengineering. Networks are by their nature inherently scaleable; they can be extended both on a local site and to remote sites without any requirement to change the network architecture. However, the servers and host systems that may be connected to the network are not always so scaleable.

Let us consider a typical scenario where lack of scaleability can cause significant problems. A business department has developed a custom application using a standard multi-user PC database product, e.g. dBase. This application happily serves 15 users on a 386-based NetWare file server. The department is expanding, and now needs to extend the network to server 50 users with the same application, ten of which are on remote sites. The file-sharing architecture on which the custom application is based will not support 50 concurrent users, and does not operate satisfactorily over wide area connections.

A considerable amount of time has been expended in writing this application. The department is faced with the choice of very slow response times to the 50 users, or rewriting the application from scratch in a more powerful database development environment running on a minicomputer or Unix supermicro. Neither of these choices are particularly satisfactory; rewriting the application will become inevitable, but will take significant time and money.

Fortunately, there are ways to avoid running into this type of brick wall. All multiuser applications requiring a significant degree of programming effort should be written using an SQL DBMS such as Informix or Oracle, in conjunction with 4GL development tools to ensure maximum development productivity. Such an application can be easily moved from a low-cost 386 Unix platform to a powerful minicomputer or RISC-based supermicro as the number of system users increases. Achieving satisfactory response times for 50 users is simply a function of providing a more powerful hardware platform.

Because of their excellent scaleability, Unix-based systems are appropriate platforms for small-to-medium scale database applications in the five to 50 transaction per second range. Beyond this point, specialised multiprocessing Unix systems (from vendors such as Pyramid and Sequent) have been benchmarked at transaction processing throughputs of over 100 transactions per second.

Other Important Factors

Successful systems implementation also depends crucially on three vital non-technological factors:

- The quality of project management in the implementation phase

- The level of positive user participation achieved

- The activities within the business that are selected for automation

This final factor is often overlooked. To achieve maximum payback from integrated network systems, you must first of all focus on identifying the critical success factors that really make a difference to the business bottom line. No matter how meticulously and effectively an activity is automated, no matter how good the technology selected for its implementation, all this will count for nothing if that activity is of secondary importance to the success of the business.

Most battles are won before they are fought. Networking projects are no exception to this rule. If due attention is not paid to network architecture issues, your network will not provide the required connectivity to other systems, and will be unmanageable. If reliability issues are not addressed in the planning phase, your network downtime will be high, and it will be very costly to engineer in the required reliability level later. If ease of use is not considered early on, your network will not win widespread user acceptance. And if your system is not scaleable, you will be faced with the need to redesign and rebuild your network as usage and traffic levels increase.

CHAPTER 9

CASE STUDIES

The case studies in this chapter are derived from Ives & Company client projects in three different industry sectors.

Client A: Foods Sector

Our client was a major supplier of fresh produce (fruit and vegetables) and prepared fresh foods, operating in a number of countries, principally within Europe. With the traditional national boundaries between food markets eroding as 1992 approaches, they faced the challenge of extending a dominant UK market position into Europe.

Those divisions within the fresh produce distribution business that had the highest degree of vertical integration between the sources of produce and the end customer had the highest profitability. Vertical integration allows a margin to be taken at each stage of the distribution chain, and allows quality to be controlled more tightly.

The client was faced with the need to replace its ageing mainframe-based systems, which were more suited to the purely UK-based business of the past. An information network architecture was required that could provide the required connectivity between far-flung sourcing, distribution and marketing locations, and out to major customers, by providing a standardised set of network services.

As the client's business shifts to a global sourcing and marketing business, an information network was required that could link a large number (up to 40) of sourcing locations in the Southern Hemisphere with the marketing locations, principally based in Europe. Shipments of fruit and vegetables were planned to be coordinated from a sourcing operations centre, which would be linked to a European marketing operations centre, and eventually to a US marketing operations centre. Information would need to be transferred frequently and rapidly between these centres, and out to the other sourcing and marketing locations if profit margins from each consignment of produce were to be maximised.

We defined an information network architecture that would effectively support this type of geographically-dispersed shipping and distribution operation. This architecture, shown in Figure 14 overleaf, provided an overall framework for local and wide area networking in the produce businesses. It recommended that local area networks based on Unix servers and PC workstations be established in the operations centres and in head office. These would be connected to each other through public international X.25 networks.

Key services that would need to be provided on these local area networks included messaging, file transfer, terminal service and electronic data interchange (EDI). We recommended that messaging be standardised around X.400 protocols, to allow the option of either local X.400 message servers, or the use of public X.400 messaging services, depending on the size of each location and the availability of local support skills.

Other network services defined within the architecture included the following:

- Asynch terminal connectivity, based on Unix services over X.25

- File transfer based on UUCP over X.25

- Future EDI services based on EDIFACT and X.400 standards

The chosen architecture provided the desired connectivity between sourcing and marketing locations, and established a

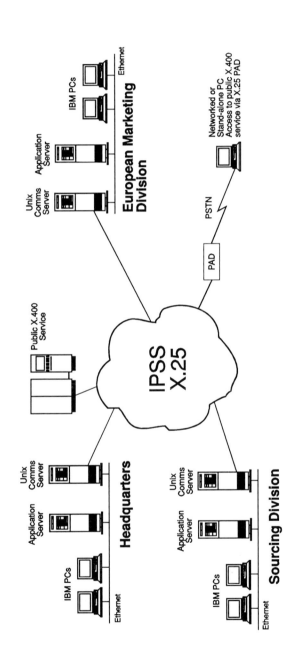

Figure 14: Foods sector client - international network

common set of network services to be provided to users worldwide. It was based on accepted and widely implemented open systems standards, including the Unix operating system, Ethernet local area networking, X.25 wide area networking and X.400 based messaging and file transfer. The architecture will allow much improved coordination and rapid response between sourcing and marketing business units, necessary to generate maximum profits from each produce shipment.

Client B: Local Government Sector

Our local government client was faced with the need to replace ageing IBM 8100-based office automation systems in central and remote sites. Its existing systems included a large IBM 3090 mainframe, over 200 PCs connected via IRMA-type coaxial connections, and a small 20 node IBM Token Ring. The local authority had also implemented a county-wide private X.25 wide area network, using SNA to X.25 protocol converters for attachment of remote PCs running 3270 emulations.

Midway through the selection process for the new office systems, the client felt that the system connectivity implications of the short-listed new systems needed to be considered in more depth. It had become apparent that any new systems would need to provide a platform for terminal connectivity and messaging services as well as the basic office automation services. We clarified the network architecture implications for both of the final short-listed systems. Once the system selection decision had been made, we defined an integrated network architecture that provided the necessary level of connectivity between the IBM mainframe systems, the new Unix-based distributed office automation systems, existing PCs and the county-wide X.25 network.

This architecture, illustrated in Figure 15, incorporated the following set of standard network services:

- Messaging, based on Unix Mail, with a future migration path to X.400

- 3270 terminal connectivity, based on 3270/QLLC protocols over X.25

- Asynch terminal connectivity, based on Telnet protocols

- NFS and TCP/IP protocols for local area networking

A key benefit of the architecture was the ability to implement systems in both the large central site (with over 1,000 staff), and small remote sites (with as few as six staff) around a consistent open systems and communications architecture.

Office automation systems could be scaled up from 386-based Unix systems in remote sites to a large multiprocessor Unix system on the central site, all running the same LAN protocols (TCP/IP, NFS), WAN protocols (X.25, 3270/QLLC) and office automation software (Uniplex).

Client C: Publishing Sector

Unlike the two previous case studies, which were concerned with defining an architecture for operations spanning a large number of sites, this study required a large local area network of approximately 400 nodes to be designed for two buildings on adjacent sites. In addition, the network had to be implemented with a high degree of fault tolerance, given the extremely tight weekly deadlines for the production of a 500-page magazine.

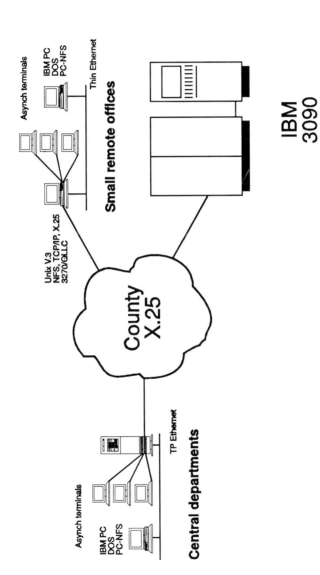

Figure 15: Local government client - county-wide network

The IT strategy of the business mapped out a system replacement program, involving the introduction of electronic publishing systems for in-house page makeup and pagination. There was a requirement for subsequent integration of those systems with commercial and office automation systems, and interconnection with three remote sites.

Existing information systems include a proprietary PDP-11 based ad booking system, and IBM System/38-based commercial systems. The lack of integration between these two systems, and the lack of extensibility of the application software was making it difficult to deliver important management reporting information. Moreover, the systems could not be extended to support electronic publishing requirements.

A key early challenge was to identify an electronic publishing system capable of handling the strenuous and very high volume requirements of the client. Our product research identified a suitable system from a US-based electronic publishing vendor, implemented on RISC server and workstation hardware from Sun Microsystems.

We constructed a network architecture based on open systems standards that could integrate the new production system together with commercial systems running the client's preferred future SQL DBMS. This architecture is represented in Figure 16.

To achieve the necessary level of fault-tolerance in the network, we designed a network cabling system with a high degree of resilience and redundancy. This system was based on a star-wired structured cabling system to the Ethernet 10BaseT standard. We specified mirrored network backbones, one backbone connected to a primary central data concentrator, and the second connected to a backup

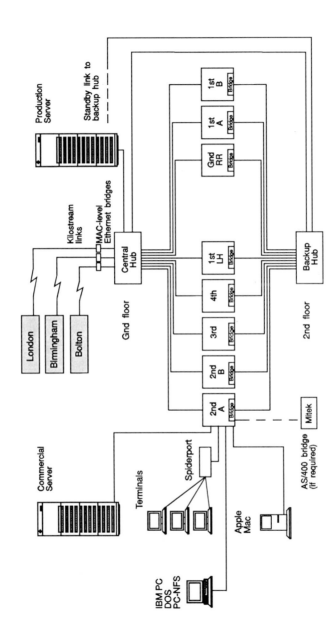

Figure 16: Publishing sector client - integrated fault-tolerant network

concentrator. The backup paths are automatically activated should there be a failure of the primary concentrator.

The network is able to survive the failure of any individual link or any individual concentrator, without losing more than 50 per cent service to the main operational production and telesales departments.

CHAPTER 10

CONCLUSION

In the brief history of computing there have been three main innovations - the transistor, the integrated circuit and the microprocessor. Out of these innovations sprang the mainframe, the minicomputer and the personal computer, respectively. Each of these spawned an entire industry to meet the demand for each new type of computing.

The Era of Integrated Networking

We are now in the midst of a transition into a fourth era of computing - the era of integrated network computing. In this era, organisations will progressively integrate their standalone host systems, PCs and local area networks into business-wide information networks. Here the stimulus is three-fold. First, the dramatic reductions in the price of computing power have made it possible to provide more and more users with their own local desktop computing resource. Second, the emergence of strong open industry standards has made it possible for the first time to build networks connecting many different types of computer. Third, the return on investment from implementing integrated business-wide systems has been shown in many studies to be significantly greater than that achieved from automating individual business processes.

Network architecture

Achieving the successful integration of existing and new systems in an organisation requires an underlying framework of standards - a network architecture.

Three principal architectures are emerging for building integrated computer environments:

- Systems Applications Architecture (SAA) - promoted by IBM

- Network Applications Support (NAS) - promoted by DEC

- Sun's Open Network Computing (ONC), backed by the majority of open systems vendors

SAA is primarily suited to corporate sites with major commitments to IBM-based mainframe and mini systems. NAS is appropriate for organisations with significant existing investments in DECnet based networks. ONC provides the most cost-effective and flexible choice for organisations that do not fall into these two categories. These are not the only architectural options to be considered. Many organisations are building information networks based on PC local area network architectures such as Novell's NetWare. Others are implementing architectures promoted by particular minicomputer vendors, e.g. HP's LAN Manager/X.

The move away from systems based on proprietary technologies to systems built around open architectures and open standards is gathering pace. This will have profound implications not only on the future structure of the computer industry, but also on how systems are implemented in organisations. Open systems are making it much easier to mix and match off-the-shelf products from different manufacturers to provide an optimal systems solution for a specific business.

The increasing diversity and complexity of computing and communications technologies is leading to an increased role for systems integrators who can 'glue' together diverse open computing and communications technologies into an integrated network system.

Integrating IT with business objectives

The challenge of defining network architectures that best support the business objectives of an organisation is leading to an increasing emphasis on the issue of information management, rather than on the information systems themselves.

Only if information is regarded as a strategic resource and managed appropriately will information technology be able to deliver the maximum return to the business.

Many of the concepts first developed to increase productivity in manufacturing environments are now finding their way into office-based service industries. Much office work today is still carried out using paper-based, batch-oriented methods that have changed little during the last 50 years.

Document image processing systems and workflow management systems are becoming the machine tools and production line of today's high volume office operations. These technologies will transform office operations in a broad range of service industries into high productivity 'office factories' with much improved levels of customer service.

Accepting networks

Ultimately the business benefits of an information network depend upon how well it is accepted by users. The responsibility of those who plan and implement network systems is very great: like architects of buildings they have an obligation to provide users with a working environment that is ergonomically sound, enjoyable to use and which can both enhance the work experience and increase efficiency. As information networks are implemented on a wider scale, this responsibility will need to be taken more seriously.

The Potential of Information Networks

If the full potential of information networks is to be realised, senior management needs to be able to combine its understanding of business strategy, business competition and business operations with a much better awareness of how information technology can be harnessed within the organisation.

Information networks promise to have such a major impact on business competitiveness in the next decade that information technology planning can no longer be relegated to a secondary position on the senior management agenda. In particular, strategic systems, which offer the greatest potential return on investment, will become a prerequisite for achieving market leadership in many industries.

APPENDIX 1

TEN GOLDEN RULES FOR SUCCESSFUL INFORMATION NETWORKING

1. Start the network planning process by attempting to identify strategic systems applications that will have the greatest impact on the bottom line.

2. Finish the process by setting quantifiable and prioritised objectives for the system before it is installed and continually track progress towards achieving these.

3. Let the quality of the software applications that are available for the business tasks at hand drive the technology selection process, not vice versa. Don't put the cart before the horse and impose technology or supplier policy decisions in a vacuum.

4. Split your budget and time allocations in a balanced way between the initial requirements analysis, the purchase of hardware and software products, the integration of these products, and training, support and software and hardware maintenance.

5. Involve the prospective users of the network in the business requirements and systems integration phases, and in the future evolution of the system.

6. Design systems that adhere to key industry standards at both the software and hardware levels.

7. Build scaleability into your system so that you won't be forced into a premature system redesign and re-integration as your processing requirements increase.

8. Design for maximum useability by implementing a consistent graphical user interface (GUI) wherever possible.

9. Design your network around departmental and central repositories of business information, that can be accessed by multiple software applications. Protect these by implementing appropriate data security procedures.

10. Design for maximum system uptime. Use high reliability components and design techniques, and implement effective backup and recovery procedures to guard against the loss of valuable business data.

APPENDIX 2

BIBLIOGRAPHY

Anderson, Ronald & Sullivan, David
World of Computing
Boston: Houghton Mifflin, 1988

Brand, Stewart
The Media Lab
New York: Viking Penguin, 1987

Healey, Martin
Case Tools are Beginning to Succeed
May 1989

Infocorp and Sanford Bernstein & Co.
Market Research Reports
1990

Ives, Stephen & Allenstein, Bernie
Office Productivity through Networking
Cambridge: Torus Systems, 1988

Judge, Peter
Open Systems: The Basic Guide to OSI and its Implementation
Sutton, Surrey: Computer Weekly Publications, 1988

Lacey, Robert
Ford - The Men and the Machine
London: Guild Publishing, 1986

Management Today
The Office Factory
July 1990

Martin, James
PC Week / Application Development Series
New York: Ziff-Davis, 1988

Nolan, Norton & Co.
The Strategic Use of PCs in Organisations
Boston: 1988

Touche Ross
The Benefits of Technology for Professional Staff
London: Touche Ross, 1988

INDEX

175

COMPUTER WEEKLY PUBLICATIONS

Computer Weekly is the UK's leading weekly computer newspaper which goes to over 112,000 computer professionals each week. Founded in 1967, the paper covers news, reviews and features for the computer industry. In addition, *Computer Weekly* also publishes books relevant to and of interest to its readership.

Publications to date (obtainable through your bookshop or by ringing (081) 661 3050) are:

COMPUTER WEEKLY GUIDE TO 300 KEY IT COMPANIES

This up-to-date, independent, analytical guide to 300 key software and hardware suppliers has been compiled to meet the demand for independent information about individual companies, which is here brought together in a highly accessible form.

The 300 companies have been selected according to a number of criteria. These include: the impact of the company within the UK, the degree of production within the UK, and the size of the company.

The late Keith Jones, who wrote about the hardware companies, was formerly European Editor of the US magazine *Mini-Micro Systems*. Phil Manchester, who has covered the software companies, was formerly Editor of the *Financial Times Fintech Software Newsletter*.

ISBN 1-85384-026-2   304 pages   A4 size   Price £65

ALIENS' GUIDE TO THE COMPUTER INDUSTRY
by John Kavanagh

In a lucid and light style, leading computer industry writer John Kavanagh discusses how the various parts of the computer industry inter-relate and what makes it tick. Complete with extensive index, the book is invaluable for all who come into contact with the computer industry.

'Business professionals who worry about their grasp of the general computing scene and do not want to be bombarded with jargon and technicalities, will get good value ... an excellent 'snapshot' of the companies, the current areas of interest and the problems' *Financial Times*

ISBN 1-85384-012-2   192 pages   A5 size   Price £9.95

COMPUTER JARGON EXPLAINED
by Nicholas Enticknap

Following reader demand this is a totally revised, expanded and updated version of our highly successful guide to computer jargon, *Breaking the Jargon*.

This 176 page book provides the context to and discusses 68 of the most commonly used computer jargon terms. Extensively cross-indexed this book is essential reading for all computer professionals, and will be useful to many business people too.

'... a useful shield against the constant barrage of impossible language the computer business throws out' *The Independent*

'... a worthwhile investment' *Motor Transport*

ISBN 1-85384-015-7   176 pages   A5 size   Price £9.95

WHAT TO DO WHEN A MICRO LANDS ON YOUR DESK
by Glyn Moody and Manek Dubash

This book will help you get the most out of your microcomputer. It is a practical book, giving advice on how to make the transition from typewriter to micro profitably and with minimum effort.

The authors look at software - wordprocessing, databases, spreadsheets, graphics and communications - and the different types of hardware on the market. The book contains valuable information on training, health and security, and legal matters including the Data Protection Act, operating systems, the history of the computer, the current micro scene and the future.

ISBN 1-85384-011-4   296 pages   A5 size   Price £14.95

CONSIDERING COMPUTER CONTRACTING?
by Michael Powell

This is a completely revised and updated edition of the highly successful book which has helped many computer professionals break loose from being employees to working freelance, in some cases doubling their salaries.

There is information on: who uses computer contractors and why; what it takes to become a contract worker; how to find your first contract; how to keep your skills updated; forming your own company and handling finances; contract agencies.

ISBN 1-85384-022-X   176 pages   A5 size   Price £12.95

HITCHHIKERS' GUIDE TO ELECTRONICS IN THE '90S
by David Manners

Developments in electronics underpin not only the computer industry but also the whole of modern society. This book is essential if DP and IT professionals are to identify trends that will affect all our jobs in the 1990s.

David Manners, an awarding winning senior editor on *Electronics Weekly* newspaper, lucidly explains the electronics industry and its key products and discusses its central role and implications to industry in the 1990s.

Essential reading for IT staff, marketing and sales directors, strategic planners and all interested in the future of the IT industry.

ISBN 1-85384-020-3   224 pages   A5 size   Price £12.95

A SIMPLE INTRODUCTION TO DATA AND ACTIVITY ANALYSIS
by Rosemary Rock-Evans

Successful analysis of business operations is a prerequisite to building any computer system within a company. Whereas many existing books approach this topic from an academic point of view, this is the fruit of years of practical analysis in blue chip companies.

Rosemary Rock-Evans is a leading consultant. Her first book on this topic for *Computer Weekly*, published in 1981, is now out of print. However, the considerable demand within the industry for this book has resulted in this totally revised and updated version.

It is essential reading for all analysts in the computer industry, and is also recommended for students to give them a taste of the real world of analysis.

ISBN 1-85384-001-7   272 pages   A4 size   Price £24.95

OPEN SYSTEMS:
The Basic Guide to OSI and its Implementation
by Peter Judge

We recognise the need for a concise, clear guide to the complex area of computer standards, untrammelled by jargon and with appropriate and comprehensible analogies to simplify this difficult topic.

This book, a unique collaboration between *Computer Weekly* and the magazine *Systems International*, steers an independent and neutral path through this contentious area and is essential for users and suppliers. It is required reading for all who come into contact with the computer industry.

ISBN 1-85384-009-2   192 pages   A5 size   Price £12.95

IT PERSPECTIVES CONFERENCE:
THE FUTURE OF THE IT INDUSTRY

Many nuggets of strategic thought are contained in this carefully edited transcript of the actual words spoken by leading IT industry decision makers at *Computer Weekly*'s landmark conference held late in 1987.

The conference was dedicated to discussing current and future directions the industry is taking from four perspectives: supplier perspectives; communications perspectives; user perspectives and future perspectives.

'... makes compelling reading for those involved in the business computer industry' *The Guardian*

'... thought-provoking points and some nice questions put to speakers at the end' *Daily Telegraph*

ISBN 1-85384-008-4   224 pages   A4 size   Price £19.95

COMPUTER WEEKLY BOOK OF PUZZLERS
Compiled by Jim Howson

Test your powers of lateral thinking with this compendium of 187 of the best puzzles published over the years in *Computer Weekly*. The detailed explanations of how solutions are reached make this a useful guide to recreational mathematics. No computer is needed to solve these fascinating puzzles.

'... a pleasant collection of puzzles exercises for computer freaks. Actually probably fewer than half the puzzles here need a computer solution ...' *Laboratory Equipment Digest*

ISBN 1-85384-002-5   160 pages   A5 size   Price £6.95

WOMEN IN COMPUTING
by Judith Morris

Written by a respected former editor of several computer magazines, this book reflects the upsurge in awareness of the important role women can play in helping to stem the critical skills shortage within the computer industry.

The book addresses women's issues in a practical and sensible way and is aimed at all business women both in the computer industry or who work with computers. Contains much practical advice, including the names and addresses of useful organisations, and a valuable further reading list.

ISBN 1-85384-004-1   128 pages   A5 size   Price £9.95

HOW TO GET JOBS IN MICROCOMPUTING
by John F Charles

As micros proliferate, opportunities for getting jobs in this area are expanding rapidly. The author, who has worked with micros in major organisations, discusses how to get started in microcomputing, describes the different types of job available, and offers tips and hints based on practical experience.

ISBN 1-85384-010-6   160 pages   A5 size   Price £6.95

LOW COST PC NETWORKING
by Mike James

The whole area of PC networking is taking off rapidly now. Can you afford to be left behind? Mike James' book shows how networking revolutionises the way we use PCs and the tasks that they perform. It also explains how networking goes further than simply linking PCs, and how it enables you to integrate your operations to transform your business.

Chapters cover every aspect of networking, from planning your network and selecting the hardware and software to applications, technicalities and contacts.

ISBN 0-434-90897-5   256 pages   246 x 188 mm   Price £16.95

SELLING INFORMATION TECHNOLOGY:
A PRACTICAL CAREER GUIDE
by Eric Johnson

Selling in IT requires more skill and creativity than selling in any other profession. This handbook explains why and provides practical down-to-earth advice on achieving the necessary extra skills. A collaboration between *Computer Weekly* and the *National Computing Centre*, this book discusses career issues, general IT sales issues, and key IT industry developments.

ISBN 0-85012-684-3   244 pages   144 x 207 mm   Price £12.50

MANAGING INFORMATION SECURITY:
A NON-TECHNICAL MANAGEMENT GUIDE
by Ken Wong and Steve Watt

This book has been written by experienced consultants in what is for most people a new field. Management issues are covered in detail. Topics include: people - are they assets or liabilities, risk assessment, devising and testing a disaster recovery plan, encryption and communication security, the impact of the PC revolution, access control, combatting hacking and viruses, and security in different vertical market sectors such as banking and retail.

ISBN 0-946395-63-2   336 pages   277 x 214 mm   Price £85

BREAKDOWNS IN COMPUTER SECURITY:
Commentary and Analysis
by Mike Rentell and Peter Jenner

Protect yourself and your company from breaches of computer security with this jargon-free compendium and discussion of over 100 genuine incidents which took place in 1988, 1989 and 1990.

Breakdowns in security have resulted in serious, sometimes fatal, injuries, and loss of considerable sums of money, sometimes leading to bankruptcy. These incidents have involved a wide range of companies, public institutions, individuals and the state

The comment on each incident will tell you what the company concerned *should* have done to prevent or alleviate the more damaging aspects of each problem.

Breakdowns in Computer Security is essential reading for all managers who have to protect their systems against accidental and malicious destruction, interference or breach of confidentiality.

ISBN 1-85384-024-6   104 pages   A5 size   Price £12.95

COMPUTER WEEKLY GUIDE TO RESOURCES 1990

Our extensively indexed second Annual Guide fulfils the computer industry's need for an independent, handy, up-to-date reference review signposting and interpreting the key trends in the computer industry.

A key section is an indepth, independent discussion of 270 software and computer companies, invaluable for managing directors, DP managers, sales and marketing people and all executive job hunters.

Our first Annual Guide was well acclaimed:

'In spite of a plethora of guides to various aspects of the computer industry, there hasn't been one readable, comprehensive overview of the current UK scene. *Computer Weekly's* Guide to Resources has filled the bill ... it's very good.' *The Guardian*.

ISBN 1-85384-017-3   416 pages   A4 size   Price £45

THE SCANNER HANDBOOK
A Complete Guide to the Use and Applications of Desktop Scanners
by Stephen Beale and James Cavuoto

Desktop scanners are quickly becoming standard components in personal computer systems. With these electronic reading devices, you can incorporate photographs and illustrations into a desktop publishing program, convert printed documents into text files, and perform advanced-capability facsimile transmission, all from the convenience of your desktop.

The Scanner Handbook is an authoritative and informative guide to selecting, installing and using a desktop scanner. In lively and entertaining prose, the authors describe the essential features of desktop scanners and explain how best to apply scanning hardware and software.

ISBN: 0-434-90069-9   256 pages   232 x 156 mm   Price £19.95

DATABASE MANAGEMENT SYSTEMS
Understanding and Applying Database Technology
by Michael M. Gorman

The next DBMS generation is here. It contains DBMSs that look alike - on the outside. This does not mean all DSMSs are the same on the inside. On the inside they perform very differently - some slow, others fast; some rudimentary, others advanced. this book is about the critical DBMS differences.

Michael Gorman goes to considerable length to detail the components of a sophisticated DBMS and to provide DBMS users and evaluators the information they need to look critically at DBMS products. He covers batch, network and relational DBMSs that operate on mainframes, minicomputers and microcomputers.

Gorman starts with a discussion of database standards. He continues with DBMS applications and components. This includes application classification, static and dynamic relationships, DBMS components and subcomponents, and DBMS requirements. This is followed by a discussion of DBMS components - the logical database, the physical database, interrogation and system control.

Contents: ANSI Database Standards; DBMS Applications and Components; The Logical Database; The Physical Database; Interrogation; System Control; Keys and BNF Notation Definition; Glossary

ISBN: 0-7506-0135-3   480 pages   Hardback   Price: £40

THE SOFTWARE ENGINEER'S REFERENCE BOOK
Edited by John McDermid

This comprehensive and authoritative reference source covers the whole topic of software engineering, including the underlying science and mathematics, software development technology, software project management and principles of applications. It provides a thorough treatment of the science, principles and practice of software engineering, stressing fundamental and stable concepts as well as summarising the 'state of the art' in software engineering methods and tools. Offering pragmatic guidance and a sound understanding of the material covered, most chapters also contain a comprehensive set of references or a bibliography for further reading.

Produced by an internationally acclaimed team of experts from the UK, continental Europe and North America, the *Software Engineer's Reference Book* is aimed at practising software engineers, software project managers and consultants. The book is edited by John A McDermid, Professor of Software Engineering at the University of York and Director of York Software Engineering Ltd.

'The breadth of coverage is excellent...John McDermid is the ideal person to edit the book. He has the right blend of theory and pragmatism for such a project.' - Professor Darrel Ince, The Open University

Contents: Applicable mathematics; Fundamental computer science; Other relevant science and theory; Conventional development; Formal development; Software development management; AI/IKBS approaches; Other approaches to software development; Programming languages; The operational environment; Principles of application; Future developments for software engineering as a profession.

ISBN: 0-7506-1040-9   1032 pages   Hardback   Price £125

PROFITING FROM YOUR PRINTER:
Users' Guide to Computer Printing
by Frank Booty

This book will help users choose a suitable printer for their computer, and includes advice as to which manufacturer and model will meet their particular requirements. Prices of the printers are included to give an idea of the pricing structures and relative costs.

Also included; how to connect a printer to your system; third/fourth party maintenance aspects; paper handling; form feeding; hidden costs; desktop publishing; and the effects of networking on printers.

ISBN: 1-8584-019-X   224 pages   A5 size   Price £14.95

GETTING COMPUTER JOBS ABROAD
by Michael Powell

This book explains how to take the first step towards working abroad. The author gives general data on the computer scene, major industries and the economy in each country. Information is given about job opportunities, whether languages are required, work permits, the cost of living, taxation, housing, transport, etc.

The author also covers work opportunities for partners, and other matters which could affect their decision to join you, or bring children to live in the country, such as healthcare, political stability, attitudes to women, and educational possibilities.

The book contains a list of embassies, which will help you gather additional information of relevance to your own particular situation.

Whatever the reason for wanting to work abroad - the poor weather or lack of opportunities in Britain, a desire to earn more money, or the wish to live another type of life - this book will help you plan your next move.

ISBN: 1-85384-016-5   235 pages   A5 size   Price £14.95